Alternative Forages
for
Ruminants

Papers presented at a conference held at th
Royal Agricultural College, Cirencester, UK,
5 March 1997

Edited by
G.P.F. Lane and J.M. Wilkinson

Chalcombe Publications

First published in the United Kingdom by
Chalcombe Publications
Painshall, Church Lane, Welton,
Lincoln LN2 3LT, UK

© Chalcombe Publications 1998

ISBN 0 948617 37 3

Printed in the United Kingdom by Booksprint

Contents

FOREWORD

G.P.F. Lane

Principal Lecturer in Grass and Forage Crops
The Royal Agricultural College, Cirencester, Glos GL7 6JS UK

"Alternative Forages for Ruminants" comprises a complete record of the proceedings of a conference held on the 5th March 1997 at the Royal Agricultural College, Cirencester under the joint auspices of the British Grassland Society, the British Society of Animal Science and the Maize Growers Association. The combination of the resources of these three societies was in itself notable but the high quality of the papers presented, the excellent attendance, and the continued interest in the topics covered have prompted this compilation. Sincere thanks are due to the officials of all three societies for a successful day.

The title of the original conference was "Quality Forage for Ruminants" which bears all the hallmarks of a decision made by a committee (which is exactly what it was). The objective, as those who read on will discover, was to bring together both academic and practical farming experience of a wide range of *alternative* forages to supplement the much greater volume of knowledge of the grass crop.

The main alternative forages addressed by the contributors were the forage legumes and there is much of interest here for the legume enthusiast. Not the least of these is the extraordinarily perceptive and erudite paper by Mr Gordon Newman with which the conference began. I firmly believe that in the future, those of us who have been privileged to know and work with Gordon will regard him in the same sort of way as we now think of Sir George Stapledon or even Professor "Bobby" Boutflour. I have made his "Overview of Forage Legumes" mandatory reading for students of forage crops at the Royal Agricultural College, and I strongly commend it to you. His contribution to our understanding of these crops, particularly lucerne, has been immense and his enthusiasm infectious.

1

There is much of value in the other contributions. It was never the intention to provide a complete coverage of alternative forages, but to encourage contributions from those who felt they had something relevant to say in the context of reducing milk and livestock prices and the bovine spongiform encephalopathy (BSE) disaster, which have prompted so much interest in home-grown protein sources. We certainly received many and varied contributions and from as far afield as Italy and the Irish Republic. All were of a very high standard and have been faithfully reported. Maize, fodder beet and kale were all covered as well as the legumes.

The final session was particularly successful in my opinion. It contained contributions from Derek Gardner of Genus on the economics of forage crops and from John Bax of the Scottish Agricultural College who has created an innovative but highly repeatable system of milk production based on white clover at the College's Crichton Royal Farm in Dumfries. The great mystery remains as to why so many livestock farmers still regard clover as "too difficult".

One of the most positive developments to come out of the conference was the re-launch of the "Forage Legumes Special Interest Group" of the British Grassland Society (BGS) which has met several times since March 1997 and is continuing the process of technology transfer between research workers, farmers and the trade. New members are particularly welcome. Contact the BGS or the Royal Agricultural College.

Finally, it has to be said that those seeking all the answers about alternative forage crops will not find them here; it's not that sort of book. My promise is that if you read the parts that interest you then you may at least find out what are the relevant questions and some of the answers.

Cirencester, November 1997

Chapter 1

An Overview of Forage Legumes

G. Newman

Travellers Rest, Timberscombe, Minehead, Somerset TA24 7UK

Summary

Although legumes are able to fix their own nitrogen supply, enrich the soil N content and have a high nutritive value, their relatively insignificant role in the UK throughout the latter half of the twentieth century has been dictated more by a protected European agriculture and subsidised energy to produce cheap nitrogen fertiliser, than by economic or biological forces. As UK agriculture becomes more influenced by a more open world market, legumes will play an increasingly important role, subject to adequate commercial support. The strengths and weaknesses of clover, lucerne, sainfoin and peas are reviewed and future research requirements identified. The opportunities for supplementing legumes with other ensiled forages, in order to maximise their specific nutritional qualities, are discussed.

Introduction

It is now half a century since Stapledon assured us that ley farming, involving the use of white clover leys, would be the future hub of food production in UK. Since then, the output of cereals, mostly grown in an entirely arable rotation, has trebled, partly due to the efforts of plant breeders and the development of more effective herbicides and fungicides, but mostly to cheap N fertiliser. 'Disenchantment' is probably the most appropriate word to describe the attitude of British farmers to legumes in recent years.

The major objective in the first session of this conference is to relaunch the old 1980s legume group, then only about 30 strong, under the umbrella of the British Grassland Society, in a more orderly and timely fashion and with a larger, but equally committed membership. As over 63% of animal protein feed requirements in Europe are imported at increasing cost, amidst a prospect of lower returns, forage legumes must have a vital future role, which progressive farmers will exploit as they become more sensitive to environmental controls. The object of this paper is to remind delegates of the strengths and weaknesses of legumes in science and practice.

General observations

Agronomic factors
Using N fertiliser is like eating sugar: habit forming but giving a rapid, reliable and repeatable response. In contrast, legumes are less predictable, sensitive to climate and soil, yield less in spring, lack persistence (probably through bad management or pests), may cause bloat, are difficult to establish because the seed is small and frequently sown too late and too deep, and, apart from lucerne, lack reserves of nutrients. Red clover, sainfoin and lucerne suffer from weed competition and wheel damage. Nitrogen fixation by mycorrhiza has a metabolic cost. For example, the growth of legume seedlings denied N is only 60% of those with ample N. Once established, however, the availability of N varies, stimulating the legume when deficient and grass or weeds when in surplus. Therefore, in the presence of ample N, legumes lose some efficiency. Soil N not only affects plants, it is affected by them, so we must expect oscillation between species. The reduced leaching of N from soils under clover swards has been well established (Djurhuus and Olsen, 1996).

Economic factors
It has been estimated that a general adoption of legumes would benefit the agricultural industry by £500m per annum, but this would adversely affect the feed and fertiliser industry to the extent of £330m (Doyle and Bevan, 1996). The reduction of inorganic N requirement, together with improved animal performance could confer significant financial gains, particularly in more extensive sheep and beef systems using up to 200 kg N/ha. The longer term saving on a hill farm could amount to £60 per ha per annum with heavier lambs which grade better and so improve

income. There are no significant additional costs for plants using N fixation when compared to plants using N fertiliser (Wood, 1996).

Clover leys cannot, however, compete financially with intensive dairying using higher rates of N fertiliser, which only show an advantage on a per animal basis. Improved production per animal is insufficient to compensate for lower production per hectare. A management risk factor and the need for more expensive herbicides which are not phytotoxic to legumes must also be considered. Output in legume grazing experiments is generally equal to that from pasture receiving up to 300kgN/ha, and although confirmed with sheep in practice, this has not been achieved with dairy cows. Work at Crichton Royal Farm demonstrated that their white clover unit gave 82% of the output of the unit receiving 350 kg N/ha (Bax, 1996).

There is also a commercial problem; for example, maize and whole-crop cereals now have a seed and silage additive trade behind them, but there is little immediate prospect of this for clover. Legume enthusiasts must continue to seek support from commerce!

Nutritional factors
Although legumes have a lower digestibility than grass, the rate of decline in digestibility with advancing maturity is much slower. Legumes, with their higher proportion of soluble cell contents to cell walls, undergo a more rapid particle breakdown and digestion in the rumen, thus achieving rapid rates of rumen clearance (Waghorn *et al.*, 1989). This, in turn, allows a higher intake of dry matter in less eating and cudding time, giving longer periods for the animal to rest or, in the wild, hide. Ruminant grazing strategy appears to be to eat as fast as possible (Orr *et al.*, 1996). The energy retention efficiency of legumes is also higher than grass and, as intakes increase, the rate of decline in efficiency is greater for grass than for legumes (Cammell *et al.*, 1986).

Although there is evidence of a greater loss of N between the rumen and duodenum, the supply of non-ammonium nitrogen supply to the gut is still enhanced in legume feeding. This is supplied by an increase in microbial protein synthesis, which may, in turn, depend on an adequate supply of fermentable carbohydrate (Beever *et al.*, 1986). This is also influenced by the amino acid supply to rumen bacteria, explaining why low methionine legume silage balances low lysine maize so well.

Over 20 years ago, work at the Grassland Research Institute demonstrated unequivocally the nutritional superiority of legumes (Beever and Thorp, 1996), which has largely been ignored by the dairy industry. The increased intake and duodenal protein supply from legumes results in improved performance of beef cattle, better killing out percentage and heavier carcase weights in lambs, with improved milk yield in cows (Thomson *et al.*, 1971). Unfortunately, current nutritional research on legumes is sparse and fragmented.

The four major legumes

White clover
Although New Zealand currently exports about 4,400 tonnes of white clover seed per annum, a total of less than 700 tonnes a year is used in the UK. New cultivars, mostly bred at the Institute for Grassland and Environmental Research (IGER), Aberystwyth, and selected under grazing conditions, are now commercially available and are giving improved performance (Frame *et al.*, 1995). The optimum clover content of a sward is 30% of annual DM yield and can vary from 5% in early spring to 60% in August (Rhodes and Ortega, 1996). Periodic oscillations in the clover content of a sward indicate that the system is working well. If the clover content is static, it indicates that the grass is not obtaining the full benefit of the N fixed by the clover (Schwinning and Parsons, 1996).

Sir George Stapledon had a simple test for estimating the clover content of a sward by 'plucking' it by hand at grazing height. If the handful contained 50% of clover, sward clover content was 30% on a dry matter basis. Although the highest intakes and best animal performances were obtained from young clover, the risk of bloat decreased with flowering. Ryan (1986) in Ireland showed that, although cows produced 6% more milk from white clover pastures compared to grass fertilised with 400 kg N/ha over a three year period, output of milk per hectare was 15% lower. This result was largely borne out by work at Crichton Royal (Bax, 1996).

Clover stolons are killed by heavy treading in winter and overgrazing with sheep can be a problem. Other workers have recorded the benefit of worm casts in covering stolons to protect them from winter damage. There is a strong positive linear relationship between spring stolon length and clover yield (Rhodes and Ortega, 1996). Shading extends stolon length but reduces branching and there is a good case for a rest from grazing in July and August, which increases white clover proportions in the sward (Gooding *et al.*, 1996). Although continuous grazing encourages clover, the New Zealand practice of continuous grazing in spring and autumn but rotational grazing in summer, stimulates clover content. A combination of zero N and close grazing enhances clover content, although 50 kg N/ha applied in early spring does not depress it (Rees *et al.*, 1996). The long term secondary effects for clover survival are better with solid farm yard manure (FYM) than slurry. Organic farmers must maintain P and K in the soil if clover is to make its proper contribution. N fixation is adversely affected by low soil pH and low calcium as well as high soil N. Best practice for establishing clover into existing swards has been well researched (Collins *et al.*, 1996).

Red clover
Better adapted to acid, clay soils than lucerne and usually grown as a short ley with Italian ryegrass, red clover has a high nutritional value and high intake characteristics. Used more for conservation than grazing, red clover is the second most important legume in the UK: 3,000 tonnes of seed were sold in 1960, compared to 57 tonnes in 1994, when France was still using 1,400 tonnes (Rhodes and Ortega, 1996).

Genetic resistance to *Sclerotinia* (clover rot) and eelworm is essential (Rhodes and Ortega, 1996). A red clover break gives the best yields in a following organic wheat crop over two years (Cormack, 1996). When grazed, red clover causes bloat in cattle and at tupping time may cause fertility problems in ewes due to the oestrogenic compounds it contains. Less demanding than lucerne, red clover is a more popular forage on organic farms.

Lucerne
Thriving on well drained alkaline soils, about 12,000 ha of lucerne are currently grown in UK. Lucerne yields about 15 t DM/ha in Northern

Europe, irrespective of rainfall. On acid sandy soils, good results are obtained when seed is lime pelleted (Deinum and Eleveld, 1986). Modern varieties carry some resistance to *Verticillium* wilt and stem eelworm, and modern herbicides have almost eliminated the problem of weed competition. American work has demonstrated how vascular discoloration and stem density can be used as a check for diseases (Undersander *et al.*, 1996). The use of potassium carbonate with a roller crimper has been shown to increase wilting rate by 75% (Meredith and Warboys, 1996). Wrapped big bales are now a popular method of conservation and the importation of baled French dehydrated lucerne has confirmed that long forage has a higher digestibility than pelleted material. Lucerne is nutritionally superior to perennial ryegrass because it has a lower cell wall content and higher cell solubles, crude protein and minerals. Despite a lower organic matter digestibility, intake is 20 to 30% higher than grass, attributed to a faster rate of digestion (Beever and Thorp, 1996). Campling (1984) concluded that both sheep and cattle grew faster on lucerne than grass, but milk production of cows was similar. Lucerne silage is normally fed in the dry matter (DM) proportion of 3:1 maize:lucerne, where very high intakes have been achieved.

Sainfoin
Traditionally grown in mixed swards on the chalk downs and in the Cotswolds, which were grazed with sheep early and then cut for hay and then for seed, the virtual disappearance of sainfoin has been due to the demise of the hard working draught horse with its great nutritional demands. The land that once grew this crop now produces 10 tonnes of wheat per hectare annually, thanks to N fertiliser. Coveted by racehorse trainers, dust free sainfoin hay is now imported. Although sainfoin has a 50% improvement in the absorption of amino acids from the intestine over lucerne (Thomson *et al.*, 1971), the condensed tannins contained in sainfoin have been unable to confer their bloat protecting advantages to red clover when mixed together (Beever and Siddons, 1986).

There may be a deficit of rumen degradable protein in ruminants given high-tannin legumes, suppressing rumen carbohydrate fermentation.

Peas

The energy cost of N fixation by peas is reduced starch in the seed, when compared to cereals (Heichel, 1985). Although technically a pulse, encouraged by the EC subsidy on protein crops, plant breeders have made a great contribution to varietal improvement and it is anticipated that over 4,000 ha of winter peas will be grown in the UK in 1997. Popular modern spring varieties are Grafila, Baccara, Solara, Eiffel, Magnus and Celica. Nodulation occurs very early in growth (Sprent and Mannetje, 1996), and canopies are formed from an interlocking mass of tendrils and petioles which contribute more than 60% of the photosynthetic area, replacing the compound leaves. Resistant to downy mildew, each plant supports and is supported by its neighbours and intercepts 15% less radiation than the old leafy types, confirming that peas cut for silage at the *'mangetout'* stage, are an extremely effective nurse crop for clover leys, particularly on organic farms. Earliness facilitates harvesting (Fox and Milford, 1996).

Other legumes

The high cost of genetic improvement by gene transfer has only been economically justified for rice, maize and soya so far and so any prospect of developments in the wide range of temperate legumes is remote.

The future

Legumes will have an important part to play in the management of resources for a sustainable UK agriculture, not only because they are able to fix nitrogen, but they also tolerate the warmer, drier climatic conditions which may come with global warming. According to Sprent and Mannetje (1996), after millions of years of evolution, they have learned to keep their nodules under control! Meanwhile, we require more precise methods of measuring both the N requirements of crops and production of nitrogen by mycorrhiza, together with its energy cost. Wood (1996) suggests that an assumption of 100 to 200 kg N/ha is not good enough! It is probably far less costly to improve the efficiency of N fixation in legumes and pulses by bacterial genetic manipulation and using the crops rotationally, even as understoreys (Clements *et al.*, 1996), than to manipulate cereals to fix N. The major effects of mycorrhizal fungi on soil particle aggregation and of legume root architecture on soil structure are acknowledged but more research is required (Gijsman and Thomas, 1995). Current research indicates that undersowing maize with lucerne could have potential (Lane and Moore, 1996).

The continuing improvement in testing and breeding of cold tolerant clover varieties in UK will need to be backed up by more on-farm management demonstrations as have been carried out in Wales (Rees *et al.*, 1996) and in Scotland (Bax, 1996), which should also deal with the practical problems of establishment, sward maintenance and productivity. Although tympany or bloat occurs rarely, where it does it is frequently fatal (Bax, 1996). The genetic introduction of the condensed tannins found in non-bloating sainfoin may be a possibility (D'Mello and Macdonald, 1996), although the UK licensing of Monensin bullets to reduce rumen protozoal activity, used extensively in other parts of the world for bloat prevention, may be preferable. As the anti-nutritional factors in tannins slow down the rapid particulate degradation of legumes in the rumen, shown to be the major factor responsible for improved animal performance (Beever and Thorp, 1996), it may be wrong to introduce them. The possibility that sub-clinical bloat adversely affects productivity must not be dismissed, however.

In the conservation field, revolutionised by the advent of mechanically wrapped big bales, the development of machinery specifically designed to speed up stem wilting but minimise leaf loss, together with the introduction of bacterial silage additives containing epiphytic microflora to prevent proteolysis will be significant (Vigezzi *et al.*, 1996). The complementary nature of legumes and forage maize, both in ruminal and post-rumen digestion will continue to be exploited (Beever *et al.*, 1996), particularly as methods of protein evaluation develop.

As organic and semi-organic systems develop, the maximisation of N utilisation and minimisation of winter leaching will become paramount, possibly resulting in more spring ploughing of clover leys (Djurhuus and Olsen, 1996). The increased use of clovers in more extensive farming systems, particularly in less-favoured areas and environmentally-sensitive areas, as well as on organic farms may be supplemented by the introduction of leguminous species on nature reserves where wildfowl and game show a distinct preference for them. Dairy farmers, however, will remain unimpressed by clover-based systems whilst N fertiliser remains cheap, European milk prices are relatively high and supplementary payments are based on output rather than on method of production. This situation must change, however, in the long term, when clover becomes a precision tool rather than the blunt instrument that we currently regard it.

References

BAX, J.A. (1996) Commercial farm experience of legume based grassland dairy systems. In: Younie, D. (ed.) Legumes and sustainable farming systems. *Occasional Symposium No.30, British Grassland Society*, pp. 262-266.

BEEVER D.E. and SIDDONS R.C. (1986) Digestion and metabolism in the grazing ruminant. In: Milligan L.P., Grovum W.L. and Dobson A. (eds.) Control of digestion and metabolism in ruminants. *Proceedings VIth International Symposium on Ruminant Physiology, Banff, Canada 1984*, pp.479-497.

BEEVER D.E., DHANOA M.S., LOSADA H.R., EVANS R.T., CAMMELL S.B. and FRANCE J. (1986) The effect of forage species and stage of harvest on the processes of digestion occurring in the rumen of cattle. *British Journal of Nutrition*, **56**, 439-454.

BEEVER D.E. and THORP C. (1996) Advances in the understanding of factors influencing the nutritive value of legumes. In: Younie D. (ed.) Legumes and sustainable farming systems. *Occasional Symposium No. 30, British Grassland Society*, pp. 194-216.

CAMMELL S.B., THOMSON D.J., BEEVER D.E., HAINES M.J., DHANOA M.S. and SPOONER, M.C. (1986) The efficiency of energy utilisation in growing cattle consuming fresh perennial ryegrass or white clover. *British Journal of Nutrition*, **55**, 669-80.

CAMPLING R.C. (1984) Lucerne, red clover and other forage legumes; feeding value and animal production. In: Thomson D.J. (ed.) *Forage Legumes, Occasional Symposium No. 16, British Grassland Society*, pp. 140-146.

CLEMENTS R.O., GEORGE S., MARTYN T. and BALSDON S. (1996) Wholecrop silage from a low input clover:cereal bi-cropping system. In: Jones D.I.H., Dewhurst R., Merry R. and Haigh P.M. (eds.) *Proceedings XIth International Silage Conference*, Aberystwyth, pp.62-63.

COLLINS R.P., FOTHERGILL M. And RHODES I. (1996) Interactions between seedlings of perennial ryegrass and white clover cultivars in establishing swards. *Grass and Forage Science*, **51**, 163-169.

CORMACK W.F. (1996) Effect of legume species on the yield and quality of subsequent organic wheat crops. In: Younie, D. (ed.) Legumes and Sustainable Farming Systems. *Occasional Symposium No. 30, British Grassland Society*, pp.126-127.

DEINUM B. and ELEVELD J. (1986) Effects of liming and pelleting on the growth of lucerne on sandy soils. *Proceedings 11th General Meeting European Grassland Federation, Troia, Portugal*, pp.270-273.

DJURHUUS J. and OLSEN P. (1996) Nitrate leaching after cut grass/clover leys. In: Younie, D. (ed.) Legumes and sustainable farming systems. *Occasional Symposium No. 30, British Grassland Society*, pp.119-123.

D'MELLO J.P.F. and MACDONALD A.M.C. (1996) Anti-nutrient factors and mycotoxins in legumes. In: Younie, D. (ed.) Legumes and Sustainable Farming Systems. *Occasional Symposium No 30, British Grassland Society*, pp.208-216.

DOYLE C.J. and BEVAN K. (1996) Economic effects of legume based systems. In: Younie, D. (ed.) Legumes and sustainable farming systems. *Occasional Symposium No. 30, British Grassland Society*, pp.247-256.

FOX K. and MILFORD G.F.J (1996) Improvements in the performance of peas, beans and lupins as grain legumes for British agriculture. In: Younie, E. (ed.) Legumes and sustainable farming systems. *Occasional Symposium No. 30, British Grassland Society*, pp.52-61.

FRAME J., BAKER R.D. and HENDERSON A.R. (1995) Advances in grassland technology over the past 50 years. In Pollott G.E. (ed.) Grassland into the 21st century: challenges and opportunities. *Occasional Symposium No. 29, British Grassland Society*, pp.31-82.

GIJMAN A.J. and THOMAS R.J.(1995) Aggregate size distribution and stability of an oxysol under legume based pastures in Eastern Columbian Savannas. *Australian Journal of Soil Research*, **33**, 153-165.

GOODING R.F., FRAME J. and THOMAS C. (1996) Effects of sward type and rest periods from sheep grazing on white clover presence in perennial ryegrass/white clover associations. *Grass and Forage Science*, **51**, 180-189.

HEICHEL G.H.(1985) Forages and legumes. In: Heath M.E., Barnes R.F. and Metcalfe D.S. (eds.) *Forages: the Science of Grassland Agriculture*. Ames, Iowa State University Press, pp.66-67.

JARVIS S.C., WILKINS R.J. and PAIN B.F. (1996) Opportunities for reducing the environmental impact of dairy farming managements: a systems approach. *Grass and Forage Science*, **51**, 21-31.

LANE G.P.F. and MOORE A. (1996) Establishment strategies for lucerne. In: Younie, D. (ed.) Legumes and Sustainable Farming Systems. *Occasional Symposium of the British Grassland Society, no 30*, pp.322-323.

MEREDITH R.H. and WARBOYS I.B. (1996) The use of roll-conditioning and potassium carbonate to increase the wilting rate of lucerne (*Medicago sativa L.*) *Grass and Forage Science*, **51**, 8-12.

ORR R.J., RUTTER P.D., PENNING P.D., YARROW N.H. and CHAMPION R.A. (1996) Grazing behaviour and herbage intake rate by Friesian dairy heifers grazing ryegrass or white clover. In: Younie, D. (ed.) Legumes and sustainable farming systems. *Occasional Symposium No. 30, British Grassland Society*, pp.221-224.

POZO M., WRIGHT A., WHYTE T.K., and COLGROVE P.M. (1996) Effects of grazing by sheep or goats on sward composition in ryegrass/white clover pasture and on subsequent performance of weaned lambs. *Grass and Forage Science*, **51**, 142-154.

REES M.E., VALE J.E., JONES J.R. and SIBBALD A.R. (1996) The role of white clover in an upland sheep system. In: Younie, D. (ed.) Legumes and sustainable farming systems. *Occasional Symposium No. 30, British Grassland Society*, pp.279-280.

RHODES I. And ORTEGA F. .(1996) Progress in forage legume breeding. In: Younie, D. (ed.) Legumes and sustainable farming systems. *Occasional Symposium No. 30, British Grassland Society,* pp.62-71.

RYAN M. (1986) Milk output from white clover based versus nitrogen based dairy systems. *Proceedings 11th General Meeting European Grassland Federation, Troia. Portugal,* pp.301-304.

SCHWINNING S. and PARSONS A.J. (1996) Interaction between grasses and legumes: understanding variability in species composition. In: Younie D. (ed.) Legumes and sustainable farming systems. *Occasional Symposium No. 30, British Grassland Society,* pp.153-163.

SPRENT J.I. and MANNETJE L. (1996) The role of legumes in sustainable farming systems: Past, Present and Future. In: Younie, D. (ed.) Legumes and sustainable farming systems. *Occasional Symposium No. 30, British Grassland Society,* pp.2-14.

THOMSON D.J., BEEVER D.E., HARRISON D.G., HILL I.W. and OSBOURNE D.F. (1971) The digestion of dried lucerne and dried sainfoin by sheep. *Proceedings of Nutrition Society,* **30,** 14A.

UNDERSANDER D., GRAU C. And COSGROVE C. .(1996) Use stem density and plant health to evaluate alfalfa stands. *Hoard's Dairyman,* Sept 10,1996, 612-613.

VIGEZZI P., ROTTIGNI B.M., SALVADORI B., SAVINO P. and GIARDINI A. (1996) Effects of inoculation of a low moisture lucerne silage with *Lactobacillus plantarum* strains selected from lucerne epiphytic microflora. In: Jones E.I.H., Dewhurst R., Merry R. and Haigh P.M. (eds.) *Proceedings of XIth International Silage Conference, Aberystwyth,* pp.260-261.

WAGHORN G.C., SHELTON I.D. and THOMAS V.J. (1989) Particle breakdown and rumen digestion of fresh ryegrass and lucerne fed to cows during a restricted feeding period. *British Journal of Nutrition,* **61,** 409-423.

WEISSBACH F. (1996) New developments in crop conservation. In: Jones D.I.H., Dewhurst R., Merry R and Haigh P.M. (eds.) *Proceedings of XIth International Silage Conference, Aberystwyth,* pp.11-25.

WOOD M. (1996) Nitrogen fixation: how much and at what cost? In: Younie D. (ed.) Legumes and sustainable farming systems. *Occasional Symposium No. 30, British Grassland Society,* pp.26-35.

Chapter 2

A Farmer's View of Lucerne

F. Moffat

*John Parker Farms, Wallops Wood Farm, Droxford,
Southampton, Hampshire SO32 3QY*

Summary

*Lucerne is an integral part of the cropping and feeding on the farm,
and has been so far many years. The crop is established either in
spring with barley or alone in mid-summer, using inoculated seed.
Once established the lucerne is cut four times a year and ensiled with
an inoculant silage additive. Lucerne silage is given to dairy cows and
to sheep together with maize silage in mixed diets.*

Introduction

The first time I remember seeing lucerne growing was as a child in
Cumbria on my uncle's farm some 40 years ago, and here we are today -
it still amazes me that more farmers do not use this wonderful forage
crop. It so much complements the feeding of dairy cows as a mixed
forage in the diet.

We have grown lucerne at Droxford on chalk downland since 1977
when we started with some twenty acres and have gradually built up over
the years. At the most we grew just over 40 hectares; now we are back
to 30 hectares because of the reduction of cow numbers. The lessons
learned have been numerous and so have the mistakes, however there is
an old saying that 'a mistake is not a mistake if you learn by it'.

Establishment

The first year we started we prepared our seed bed drilled in 70 kg. barley per ha then cross-drilled, diagonally, both ways with lucerne at the rate of 16 to 18 kg per ha, the seed having already been inoculated that morning on the farm. The method we use is with water and inoculum which is mixed with the seed and allowed to dry on the barn floor for about two hours before sowing. The variety we used was Vertus, mainly because it was resistant to *Verticillium* wilt. Vertus is a variety we have used many times as it seems to have persistent growth and stays healthy. Drilling normally takes place in early to mid-May.

As we have very flinty soils it is very important to heavy roll once drilling is complete. From then on in the early growth stages we treat it as a crop of barley, with the exception of any top dressing - none is necessary. Only once have we had a problem with the barley crop and this was with so-called 'gout' fly which really affected the crop. It is very important that the barley crop is not too thick as this impedes the growth of the lucerne.

We followed this method of establishment for about 15 years until the advent of set-aside, then we began to think differently. In recent years we have changed our time of establishment to mid to late summer depending on the ruling from Brussels as to when we can plough and drill a subsequent crop after set-aside.

The first year we did this we drilled on the 15th or 16th July using just lucerne at 18 kg per ha, having previously coated the ground with plenty FYM and slurry prior to ploughing and working down. We still cross-drilled the lucerne but did not use a cover crop. The season was all in favour of growing and we cut the first cut in October the same year. More recently we have had to drill later using the same principles.

Harvesting

To continue with the establishment year first. Having grown a cover crop of barley and taken its health into account, by mid-July one ought to have the lucerne growing well within the crop and the barley getting to the 'cheesy' stage. This is then the right time to harvest the crop as a forage crop for ensiling in the normal way, making an arable silage good enough for growing youngstock or dry cows, but not to be used as a milk production ration. Usually one has already some established lucerne to cut so this is not a problem. Now that we are using a different method of establishment, all the forage from the same cut can go into the same clamp.

Traditionally once established we cut four times a year, starting in late May or by the first week of June, cutting every six weeks, in mid-July, end of August and finally in mid-October if weather and growing conditions prevail, otherwise the final crop of the year will be eaten off with sheep during mid-winter.

Cutting the crop is done with a self-propelled Heston mower, cutting two ten-foot swathes and laying them side by side with a span of no more than 4 metres, which is the header width of our self-propelled New Holland forage harvester. We have stopped crimping so we leave the swath open for drying. We have the machinery capacity to harvest between 20 and 25 hectares per day, and with good weather predictions it is possible to choose the optimum harvesting times at about six week intervals. We like to cut 36 to 48 hours before picking up with the forage harvester, weather permitting.

Having tried many variable types of silage additives from straight molasses to sulphuric acid, now comes the advert for which I make no excuse Now we are ardent users of H.M. Inoculant from Nutrimix, a product that I rate very highly.

On the early cuts of the year we test for buffer index and then we use the enzyme which does make it more expensive per tonne treated, but when I reflect how in the early days our silage was often butyric now the pH remains around 4.5 to 5 and we often carry surplus silage over to a second year without any problem. Another unwritten rule is to roll, roll and roll as we are filling the clamp with a tractor with dual wheels and woe betide anyone who does not adhere to this rule. The analysis of two samples of lucerne silage taken in 1996 is shown in Table 2.1.

We normally keep our crops down for four years before ploughing up for winter wheat, and providing one can bury the root system when ploughing and drilling the subsequent crop of wheat benefits from the lucerne and the nitrogen requirement in the first year can be reduced by some 25%.

Table 2.1   Analysis   of two samples of lucerne silage 1996, John Parker Farms

	Sample 1	Sample 2
Dry matter (DM) (g/kg fresh weight)	285	331
Crude protein (g/kg DM)	180	179
Acid detergent fibre (g/kg DM)	314	269
Neutral detergent fibre (g/kg DM)	430	365
pH	4.18	3.92
Ammonia-N (g/kg total N)	102	111
Metabolisable energy (MJ/kg DM)	10.7	11.3
Digestible organic matter in the dry matter (g/kg)	675	715

Feeding

As a forage crop, lucerne has a wide range of uses; we use it mainly in our dairy cow rations at a 3 to 1 ratio of maize to lucerne and with our youngstock from 12 weeks of age in a ratio of 2 lucerne to 1 of maize.

We find the two forages complement each other very well. In the early days before we were growing as much maize as we do today we used to cut lucerne direct in the summer and give it to the cows when we were short of grass in a dry year. Now we find it much better to use lucerne silage as a buffer feed in summer, mixed with maize silage in a complete diet feeder wagon.

We find the sheep benefit from a very similar ration to that given to the cows. We call it a 'mini-cow ration' and give it to the 650 ewes lambing in January to produce Easter lambs for sale through Chitty Lamb Group to Waitrose Ltd.

Some sample rations are shown in Table 2.2.

Table 2.2   Examples of rations based on lucerne and maize silages

Milking cow ration	**(kg/cow/day)**
Soyabean meal / rapeseed meal	4.0
Fishmeal	0.4
Regumaize	1.0
Sodagrain (sodium-hydroxide treated wheat)	5.0
Whole cotton seed cake	2.0
Minerals	0.3
Maize silage / lucerne silage	3:1 ratio

Sheep ration	**(kg/head/day)**
Soyabean meal / rapeseed meal	0.75
Soda spelt (sodium-hydroxide treated spelt)	1.00
Molasses	0.25
Maize silage / lucerne silage	2:1 ratio

In conclusion, we now have a very integrated system with lucerne playing a vital role in the feeding of animals and in the production of milk and meat in a way that helps us control our production costs.

Chapter 3

A Novel Technique for Establishing Lucerne (*Medicago sativa*) by Undersowing in Forage Maize

G.P.F. Lane

*The Royal Agricultural College, Cirencester,
Gloucestershire GL7 6JS UK*

Summary

The results of previous small plot studies are summarised and used to create guidelines for undersowing lucerne into established forage maize. A field-scale study is described where lucerne seed was drilled into an established maize crop shortly after spraying with bromoxynil for the control of broad leafed weeds. In spite of exceptionally dry conditions the lucerne seedlings established well and a satisfactory plant density was observed after maize harvest. Physical damage to the seedlings during a dry harvest period was minimal. However, in wet conditions a greater level of damage to young seedlings was predicted.

Introduction

Lucerne has become an established part of the forage area at the Royal Agricultural College's Coates Manor Farm and the area sown to lucerne has gradually expanded to the present 20 hectares. The combination of the soil type (Sherborne Series Cotswold Brash) and the low level of summer rainfall (10-year average: 322 mm between April and September) make lucerne an ideal choice both as a crop for conservation as silage or hay or for zero-grazing during severe drought periods. Soil moisture deficits under grass often exceed 100 mm during the summer months, and during the summer of 1996 remained at about 120 mm from late June until late September. In such circumstances grass growth is negligible, and without the contribution of lucerne, the forage supply for the College dairy herd of 160 cows would be in severe jeopardy.

Small plot studies

The main problem associated with lucerne growing, and the main reason why it has not achieved a greater degree of popularity concerns its speed of establishment. Lucerne has often been spoken of as a "difficult" crop to establish. This has not been our experience. The crop itself is quite easy and straightforward to establish. It just takes rather a long time. Field trials carried out in 1995 and 1996, in which various establishment strategies for lucerne were compared, indicated that establishment in the period between late April and early June was best and that direct sowing rather than undersowing was best from the point of view of the number of plants established per square metre (Lane and Moore, 1996; Lane and Moore, 1998). Undersowing in forage maize offered significant advantages however, achieving reasonably good levels of establishment but also offering the possibility of a valuable additional forage yield from the maize during the establishment year. Lucerne undersown in spring barley, although reasonably successful was badly affected by the dry conditions in 1995 and this gave rise to a significantly smaller number of plants and a significantly lower yield during the first harvest year (1996).

Lucerne sown later in 1995, between July and September (e.g. after winter barley), as has been the practice on Coates Manor Farm for some years, failed to establish in the extreme drought of that year. It has been our experience that later sown lucerne often gives disappointing yields (8 to 9 tonnes of dry matter per hectare) during its first harvest year. Conversely, spring sown lucerne was shown to give excellent yields in the first harvest year (up to 12 to 13 tonnes of DM/ha from three cuts in 1996) in spite of the drought (Lane and Moore, 1998).

A field-scale establishment study

The experience reported above was encouraging and, in view of the fact that forage maize now forms an equally important part of the forage area for conservation, it was decided to try to establish lucerne by undersowing in forage maize on a field scale in 1996.

This study took place in field 28 ("West Field") of Coates Manor Farm. As with the previous small plot trials the soil type was Sherborne series Cotswold Brash. The previous cropping had been winter barley followed by rape/forage turnips which had been grazed by sheep. The field received a light dressing of slurry from the dairy herd and was ploughed on 16th February 1996. After rolling, a seedbed was produced for the maize using a "Triple K" cultivator shortly before precision sowing. A total of 85 kg N and 45kg P_2O_5/ha was applied. A crop of forage maize (cv Azis) was successfully established at about 110,000 seeds/ha on 25th April 1996. The variety Azis was thought to be ideal since it is one of the earliest available. Although a later-maturing variety would almost certainly have given a higher yield of maize it was felt desirable to minimise crop competition and potential damage to the lucerne plants at harvest by using an early-maturing hybrid.

Weed control
Obviously weed control strategy was an integral part of the operation. In common with a great many other maize growers, atrazine has normally been used at the College as a residual herbicide to control spring-germinating broad-leafed weeds. Since the use of atrazine would have precluded a successful undersowing operation, it was instead decided to use bromoxynil ("Bromatril P") post weed emergence. Since bromoxynil has no residual effects it would be safe to sow the lucerne seed after spraying. Bromatril P was sprayed on to the study area at 2.11 1/ha on 13th June. The main weed problems were fat hen (*Chenopodium album*) and red deadnettle (*Lamium purpureum*) with a small amount of annual grass weeds (mainly *Poa* spp). There was also a small amount of common couch (*Elymus repens*) evident at the field margins. At the time of spraying the weeds were well established and the maize plants had about five leaves. In spite of being quite big the broad leafed weeds were reasonably well controlled by the herbicide.

Sowing the lucerne seed

Having first been inoculated with a culture of *Rhizobium meliloti*, the lucerne seed (cv Vela) was sown on 17th June into the established maize crop using an "Accord" 4 m pneumatic seed drill, at approximately 20 kg/ha. The action of the drill and the light tined harrow attached to it was sufficient to cover the majority of the seed at about 1 cm and to give a valuable additional physical treatment to the weeds which had already been badly scorched by the herbicide. In the previous plot study the lucerne seed had been broadcast by hand and covered in using a "Tearaway Weeder" finger tine harrow. Both techniques proved to be equally suitable. However the possibility of running over the maize plants during field operations would favour the use of one pass with a drill as described above as it reduced the likelihood of physical damage. A broadcasting operation would have necessitated two passes through the maize crop with additional potential for wheel damage.

Field observations

Although weed control was by no means perfect, it was felt to be adequate and weeds did not present a major challenge to either the maize or the young lucerne plants. Chickweed (*Stellaria media*) developed in parts of the undersown area as well as annual grass weeds (mainly *Poa* spp.) and common couch at the field margins. Both of these problems could be controlled by the use of an autumn application of carbetamide ("Carbetamex") which was very successful in the plot study in the autumn of 1995.

Pest damage to the young lucerne plants was minimal. This was in contrast to the previous year's study when pea and bean weevil (*Sitona lineatus*) had been a major problem requiring up to three applications of deltamethrin for satisfactory control. No evidence of weevil damage or any other significant pest, was seen in this study area.

In spite of very dry conditions the lucerne plants established quickly and grew quite well and an average of 146 plants/square metre was counted after maize harvest in October. It was a matter of some interest that in spite of large cracks appearing in the soil and a soil moisture deficit of about 120 mm the lucerne seedlings had appeared to be under little stress. The main concern was the possibility of severe physical damage to the seedlings during maize harvest. This proved to be minimal in the very dry conditions obtaining around 20th October 1996. With a later harvest and/or wetter soil conditions more serious damage might ensue. Oversowing damaged areas with red clover (*Trifolium pratense*) as recommended by Sheldrick *et al.* (1994) would be one way of alleviating such damage and this has been practised with some success on one of the current lucerne stands on the College farms.

Conclusions

Undersowing lucerne in forage maize after spraying with bromoxynil appears to be a viable technique for the Cotswolds. An early-maturing maize hybrid is thought to be essential as well as some form of physical cultivation after sowing to cover the seed. Lucerne established well under forage maize and seedling damage during a dry maize harvest period was minimal. The same principles could be applied for undersowing other crops (e.g. grasses) in forage maize and there is currently some evidence that this is already happening (Burns, 1996).

Acknowledgement

The author acknowledges with thanks the cooperation of the Farms Director, Michael Limb, the Farms Manager Tony Norris, and Paul Thompson, who all provided valuable advice and managed to find time to go the extra mile in order to assist this study. The contributions of Adrian Moore and Christine Lees to the original plot study and the donation of seed by DLF Trifolium, Tetbury, are also gratefully acknowledged.

References

BURNS J. (1996) "Undersown maize looks an antidote to pollution", *Farmers Weekly*, 1st November 1996.
LANE G.P.F. and MOORE A. (1996) Establishment strategies for lucerne. In: Younie, E. (ed.) Legumes and sustainable farming

systems, *Occasional Symposium No 30, British Grassland Society,* pp. 322-323.

LANE G.P.F. and MOORE A. (1998) The effect of establishment method and spring plant populations on the yield of a first season stand of lucerne (*Medicago sativa*). In: Lane G.P.F. and Wilkinson J.M. (eds.) *Alternative Forages for Ruminants.* Chalcombe Publications, UK.

SHELDRICK R.D., NEWMAN G and ROBERTS D.J (1995) *Legumes for Milk and Meat.* Chalcombe Publications, UK.

Chapter 4

Green Crop Drying

B. Wightman[1]

Hanford plc, Hanford Farms, Bourne Park,
Piddlehinton, Dorchester DT2 7TU

Summary

The Hanford Farms green crop drying enterprise includes both grass and lucerne crops. The grass crops receive slurry from a large pig enterprise, while the lucerne is a complementary source of forage for the dryer which is drought-resistant. The important features of dried green crops in the diet of ruminants are their relatively high contents of digestible fibre, undegraded protein and beta carotene. The fibre in dried green crops buffers acidity in the rumen and their inclusion in the diet improves output of milk from home-produced feeds.

Introduction

Aid for dehydrated forage was introduced in 1974/75 because:-

1) There is a shortage of animal feed protein in the European Union.

2) Green forage crops for dehydration contributed to the improvement of soil fertility, the prevention of soil erosion and water losses through natural drainage. The crops retained nitrates which would otherwise be lost from the soil. In some regions grains and forage crops were an essential part of the crop rotation where land was otherwise used for continuous cereal production.

---

[1] Present address: 6 Old Brickfields, Broadmayne, Dorchester, Dorset, DT2 8UY

Why did Hanford Farms get involved in green crop drying? Initially large areas of grass were grown, then lucerne for the reasons mentioned above. **Dried lucerne and grass are natural feeds, produced without additives, and are free of harmful bacteria because of the high temperature drying process. They also confer benefits to animal health, general well being and fertility**. As the Hanford pig operation expanded and with it the volume of slurry, the lucerne area was reduced. The lucerne did not need the nutrient value of regular applications of slurry neither did it like to have heavy vehicles travelling on it continually. We kept the maximum possible area down to lucerne to provide material in dry periods when the grass (tall fescue) might have been struggling. The lucerne balanced our rotation of cereals when we were growing the maximum to satisfy our pig operation.

The benefits of dried grass in ruminant feeds may be summarised as follow:

- A natural buffer to changes in rumen pH when concentrates are given, with reduced risk of acidosis, better digestion of forage by rumen microbes and improved milk production from home grown bulk feeds.
- Less degradation of protein in the rumen and a valuable source of undegraded protein.
- A rich source of beta-carotene, shortages of which can lead to cystic ovaries, weak signs of oestrus, and lower conception rates.

History has a habit of repeating itself and whilst preparing for this presentation I noticed in our lucerne file minutes of a meeting held at Rothamsted Experiment Station on 21 November 1986 to consider the relative neglect of lucerne in the UK compared with other European countries. In attendance, amongst others, were Gordon Newman and John Alliston. Gordon drew attention to the particular value of lucerne for milking cows and racehorses. Here we are 11 years on and still discussing it! The British Association of Green Crop Dryers (BAGCD) has actively been marketing the virtues of "de-hy" products in the last twelve months but dare I suggest coming from behind rather than leading. We will continue to grow crops for drying and are looking to expand the area grown as and when land becomes available. Our commitment to the product has been strengthened by demand for our finished products following the BSE crisis, because of farmers' realisation of the value of green crop forages, and of course we have never used meat and bone meal.

Fresh grass and lucerne are natural feeds for ruminants. They are the crops ruminants have evolved to eat - the forages their digestive systems utilise most effectively. It follows that British high temperature dried grass and dried lucerne are also natural feeds for ruminants. The high temperature drying process evaporates the moisture from the fresh material in a matter of seconds, not only sterilising it and making it safe to store, but also producing a feed that retains virtually all the nutritional value of the crop from which it was made. In fact, the high drying temperature has a beneficial effect on the protein content by reducing its degradability in the rumen (ERDP) and increasing the amount available for digestion in the small intestine (DUP). High temperature dried grass and dried lucerne are produced from crops that are cut and harvested at the optimum stage of growth. They are **not** by-products. They are natural, high quality feeds of vegetable origin which are totally safe to feed and have a unique role in modern high performance ruminant diets.

The crops

Hanford's grass crops are grown specifically for drying. The grass is cut 4 to 5 times per year to obtain material of a consistent and high nutritional value. The harvested crop is 'flash-dried' through the Hanford Swiss-Combi drier at Bourne Park. Grass is fed through a rotary drum along with a high volume of air at 800°C. The moisture of the grass is reduced to 12% within 45 to 90 seconds, depending on initial moisture content. The resultant dried product is milled and cubed.

The principal species used for grass drying is tall fescue, which is ideally suited to the process. Lucerne is usually cropped for three years as part of an arable rotation. Unlike grass, lucerne has the advantage of not requiring nitrogenous fertiliser after each cut as it fixes its own nitrogen from the atmosphere. Swaths are normally allowed to wilt in the field for a few hours before being picked up with a forage harvester and hauled to the dryer.

The drying process

The harvested crop is dried in a rotary drum dryer. Fresh material is fed into one end of the drum through which is drawn a high volume of air at about 800°C. As the material passes through the rotating drum, the moisture is evaporated and reduced to approximately 12 per cent in 45 to 90 seconds, depending on the initial crop moisture content. The dried material is then usually milled and pelleted before being cooled ready for storage, but some producers leave it in its chopped form to provide long fibre material that is ideal for stimulating rumen function in high yielding dairy cows.

Dried grass has a relatively high fibre level which, unlike straw, is highly digestible and has a beneficial effect in helping to balance rumen volatile fatty acid production and to buffer high starch feeds.

The typical composition of dried grass, dried lucerne and selected other ruminant feeds is shown in Table 4.1.

Table 4.1   Typical composition of dried grass, dried lucerne and selected other feeds for ruminants

	Grass silage	Barley grain	Molassed sugar beet feed	Barley straw	Dried grass 4-star	Dried lucerne 4-star
Metabolisable energy (MJ/kg DM)	11.0	13.3	12.5	7.0	11.0	9.0
Crude Fibre (g/kg DM)	270	46	129	430	184	260
Neutral cellulase digestibility (g/kg DM)	700	887	860	420	710	650
Neutral detergent fibre (g/kg DM)	490	201	322	810	536	465

Chapter 5

The Use of Artificially Dried Lucerne in Dairy Cow Diets

R.H. Phipps, A.M. Cocker and A.K. Jones

Centre for Dairy Research, Department of Agriculture, The University of Reading, Arborfield Hall Farm, Arborfield, Reading RG2 9HX

Summary

Sixteen multiparous cows received a complete diet (60:40 forage concentrate ratio). The forage components were grass silage (GS) alone (T1), maize silage (MS) and GS in a 2:1 DM ratio (T2), MS and high temperature dried lucerne (DL) in a 2:1 DM ration (T3), or feeds as in T3 but with MS and DL treated prior to feeding with a cell wall degrading enzyme (T4). The crude protein, neutral detergent fibre, starch and metabolisable energy content for GS, MS and DL were 157, 84 and 215; 468, 413 and 420; 243, trace and trace g/kg DM and 10.7, 11.7 and 10.2 MJ/kg DM, respectively. The DM intakes and milk yields for T1, T2 , T3 and T4 were 18.0, 20.3, 21.0 and 20.3 and 28.2, 28.6, 30.0 and 29.0 kg/day. The inclusion of DL increased both DM intake (P<0.01) and milk yield (P<0.05) when compared with GS, with intermediate values for the GS/MS mixture. Milk fat and protein contents for T1, T2, T3 and T4 were 46.5, 46.1, 40.7 and 43.0 g/kg and 31.6, 32.4, 32.8 and 31.9 g/kg, respectively. The inclusion of DL reduced (P<0.05) milk fat and increased milk protein content when compared with GS, with intermediate values for the MS/GS mixture.

Introduction

The role of mixed forage diets in dairy production has been the subject of a major research programme at CEDAR and has resulted in the broad acceptance of using forage mixtures rather than a single forage source. The most popular forage mixture was based on maize and grass silages. However, wherever maize silage is successfully used it is often in combination with lucerne. Unlike mainland Europe where lucerne is grown extensively, the area grown in the UK is small. The nutritional attributes of lucerne, coupled with improved production and conservation techniques suggest that its role in dairy production systems should be re-evaluated. The aim of the current study was to determine the effect of forage mixtures of maize silage and either grass silage or dried lucerne on feed intake and milk production of lactating dairy cows, and to examine the effect of enzyme application to maize and lucerne at the time of feeding.

Materials and methods

Sixteen multiparous cows were used in a 4 x 4 Latin square design, with four-week periods. The forage component of the complete diets constituted 60% of DM and contained, grass silage (GS) alone (T1), maize silage (MS) and GS in a 2:1 DM ratio (T2), MS and high temperature dried lucerne (DL) (T3) and MS and DL treated prior to feeding with a cell wall degrading enzyme[1] (T4). The enzyme was applied to the forage at 2 l/t DM prior to feeding. The diets were formulated to be isonitrogenous and isoenergetic. Levels of inclusion of the straights and compound in the diet are shown in Table 5.1.

Results

Results presented in Table 5.2 show that DM intake for T1 (18.3 kg/day) was lower (P<0.01) than the other three treatments, which were not significantly different from each other. The milk yield of 30.0 kg/d

---

[1] Finnfeeds International Ltd

recorded for T3 was higher when compared with the 28.2 and 28.6 kg/d recorded for T1 (P<0.01) and T2 (P<0.05) respectively. There was no significant difference in DM intake and milk yield when comparing T2 and T4. The milk fat contents for T1 and T2 were markedly higher when compared with T3 (P<0.01) and T4. Although the inclusion of maize silage in T2 reduced milk fat content when compared with T1, and the inclusion of the enzyme additive to the lucerne-based diet increased milk fat content in T4, the differences were not significant. The milk protein content for T3 was higher (P<0.01) when compared with T1 with an intermediate value recorded for T2. The protein yield of 982 g/d in T3 was higher (P<0.01) than the other three treatments.

Table 5.1   Inclusion rate of straights and compound in complete diets (% of total diet DM)

| | Treatments | | |
	T1	**T2**	**T3 and T4**
Soybean meal	1.9	4.2	1.9
Rapeseed meal	4.2	4.2	4.2
Regumaize	0	7.1	4.2
Compound (180g CP/kg DM)	33.5	23.2	28.8

Table 5.2   Feed intake, milk yield, composition and yield of milk constituents

| | Treatments | | | | |
	T1	**T2**	**T3**	**T4**	**s.e.d.**
Feed intake (kg DM/day)	18.0	20.3	21.0	20.3	0.64
Milk yield (kg/day)	28.2	28.6	30.0	29.0	0.56
Milk composition (g/kg)					
Fat	46.5	46.1	40.7	43.0	1.56
Protein	31.6	32.4	32.8	31.9	0.35
Yield of milk constituent (g/day)					
Fat	1312	1322	1226	1249	48.6
Protein	887	921	982	919	20.8

Discussion and conclusions

The increase in total DM intake of 2 kg/d when MS replaced 660 g/kg of GS confirms earlier studies at CEDAR. However, the use of DL further increased DM intake by 0.7 kg/d and confirms its high intake potential which supports studies from other countries. Although the inclusion of MS in a GS based diet increased feed intake, milk yield did not respond, but milk protein content increased from 31.6 to 32.4 g/kg. Studies have indicated that when MS replaces GS either milk yield or milk protein content increases, rarely both, but that the yield of milk protein was invariably increased. The current results show that not only did DM intake and milk yield respond when cows were offered a diet based on MS and DL but that milk protein content was also increased significantly. The responses resulted in a 95 g/d increase in protein yield when compared with cows offered a diet based on GS as the sole forage, and 62 g/d increase when compared with a MS/GS based diet. Increased milk yield and improved milk protein content resulting from the inclusion of DL in dairy cows diets has been noted in the literature. While the inclusion of MS in the GS based diet produced only a small depression in milk fat the inclusion of DL caused a highly significant depression in milk fat synthesis (Treatment T3). This result agrees with reports in the literature. The cause of the milk fat depression is thought to be associated with the relatively low NDF value of DL and also that its inclusion influences rumen fermentation resulting in higher concentration of propionate, which is associated with lower milk fat and higher milk protein content. The results of the current study demonstrate that dried lucerne has the potential to be a valuable ration ingredient in dairy cows diets. Comparison of treatments T3 and T4 revealed that addition of the cell wall degrading enzyme to the forages at the lower feeding had no effect on either feed intake or milk production.

Acknowledgements

The authors thank Dengie Crops Ltd and Finnfeeds International Ltd for financial support.

Chapter 6

The Potential of White Clover

A. Hopkins

*Institute of Grassland and Environmental Research,
North Wyke Research Station, Okehampton, Devon, EX20 2SB*

Summary

*White clover (***Trifolium repens***) is the main forage legume in the UK, grown in long-term grass/clover swards managed primarily for grazing. Herbage production from grass/white clover without fertiliser N is typically 5 to 10 t DM/ha, similar to grass receiving over 200 kg N/ha. Compared with grass, white clover has superior feed value, higher intake, and can maintain digestibility for longer, resulting in higher individual animal performance, but at lower stocking rates compared with heavily N-fertilised grass. Greatest benefits are with sheep, followed by beef and dairying. The benefits of white clover can confer significant financial gains to farmers, particularly when compared with moderately high fertiliser-N systems. The role of white clover in the UK is vastly below its potential, due to perceptions of risk, variations in production and unfamiliarity of management. In the long term economic necessity will force greater adoption of legumes.*

Introduction

In the United Kingdom, and in many other temperate regions of the world, white clover is the most important forage legume on account of its suitability for a wide range of situations, relatively good persistency, high feed value and its role in nitrogen fixation. Clover has been used to improve pastures since at least the early 1600s (Fussel, 1964) and earlier this century clover-rich pastures were highly valued for fattening cattle and lambs. In the post-war expansion of British agriculture legumes went out of favour, particularly in the lowlands, as nitrogen fertilisers were adopted in conjunction with grass leys as an easy and reliable means of achieving high grassland output. Interest in the potential of white clover was renewed after the energy price rises in the 1970s, amid concerns about the wisdom of reliance on fossil fuels to support agriculture. During the past decade interest in legumes has been further increased by environmental concerns and by demands for less intensive and more sustainable farming systems. Evolving reforms of the Common Agricultural Policy (CAP) and the Common Agreement on Tariffs and Trade (GATT) will mean that, in the future, livestock producers will need to reduce input costs if profitable production is to be maintained. It is opportune to consider how white clover might help achieve this.

Productivity of white clover swards

Published data on the productivity of white clover relate primarily to grass/white clover swards (usually with perennial ryegrass), the production potential of the mixture being greater than for pure white clover. Most data are derived from cutting trials which attempt to simulate (albeit unsatisfactorily) the defoliation management of rotational grazing. Herbage production is typically 5 to 10 t DM/ha, with values at the lower end of the range being on sites subject to adverse growing conditions such as moisture stress, or from swards with a low proportion of clover. The white clover in grass/clover swards can, through its associated root rhizobia, fix nitrogen at rates reported to be up to 280 kg N/ha in lowland swards (Cowling, 1982) and up to 150 kg N/ha in upland swards (Newbould, 1982). These values are based on a white clover proportion of about 25% on a dry matter basis.

Perennial ryegrass swards receiving maximum rates of fertiliser N (e.g. 400 kg N/ha) are capable of 12 to 15 t DM/ha on good grass-growing sites (Hopkins *et al.*, 1995). However, average rates of fertiliser N application on permanent grassland in Britain are less than 150 kg N/ha (Chalmers *et al.*, 1992). Surveys have shown that white clover is either absent or is a minor sward component in the majority of swards

(Hopkins *et al.*, 1988), and it clearly has the potential to replace all or some of the fertiliser N on a high proportion of grassland.

Feeding value of white clover

The nitrogen fixation value of white clover is well known, and in the uplands and on some organic farms this may be the main requirement. Its contribution to improving the nutritive value of forage is less well appreciated, but is probably of even greater importance to British agriculture generally. The higher nutritive value of legumes relative to grasses was shown conclusively by Ulyatt *et al.* (1977), and more specifically for white clover by Thomson (1984). The high protein content and low structural fibre of white clover, compared with that of most pasture grasses, leads to improved digestion, associated with faster rates of particle breakdown and more efficient utilization of nutrients. Unlike grasses, or legumes such as lucerne and red clover, white clover maintains its digestibility value as it matures because there is little stem development and old leaves are continually replaced. This has two effects: digestibility of the whole sward is kept high and the rate of decline is slow.

Animal production responses are influenced not only by forage nutritive value but also by intake. In general, ruminants offered legumes *ad libitum* consume 20 to 30% more than grass of similar digestibility. This advantage has been shown for sheep and cattle, and with both fresh and preserved forages. The rate of particle breakdown and the passage of feed in and from the rumen is faster with white clover than with perennial ryegrass (Mosely and Jones, 1984). Also, intake on white clover swards can be higher because animals spend less time biting and chewing than they do on grass-only swards.

Livestock production from white clover

Numerous reviews of grazing studies have been published showing the benefits of including white clover in the sward. Greatest benefits have been shown with sheep; in particular weaned lambs in late summer when the contributions of white clover in the sward is highest (Table 6.1).

Output per hectare from sheep grazing grass/white clover has been shown to be higher than that from the top one-third of MLC sheep producers, who used 165 kg N/ha on average, (Newton and Davies, 1987), and a greater proportion of lambs was also finished to required live weights and carcase conformation (85% for grass/clover vs. 50% for grass alone). White clover in the diet of lactating ewes has also been shown to increase lactation and lamb growth without depletion of ewe body reserves (Gibb and Treacher, 1983 and 1984).

Table 6.1   Daily lamb growth rate (g/day) on grass/white clover and N-fertilised grass (200 kg N/ha) pastures at an upland and lowland site (Davies and Munro, 1988)

	Liveweight gain (g/day)			
	Pre-weaning		Post-weaning	
	Grass/clover	Grass	Grass/clover	Grass
Upland	201	186	112	86
Lowland	232	212	140	81

Experiments with beef cattle have shown that stocking rates on clover-rich swards were about 75 to 80% of those achieved on grass receiving 180 to 400 kg N/ha and differences in individual animal liveweight gains were small, resulting in output per hectare being c. 80% that of high-N fertilised grass (Clark, 1988). Research at IGER has demonstrated successful production of beef from grass/white clover forage, in an 18-month system. Steers grew at 0.7 kg/day on grass/clover silage before turn-out, 0.8 kg/day during grazing, and 1.0 kg/day finishing on silage. Overall stocking rate was 3.3 cattle/ha, giving over 1000 kg/ha output at very low cost without supplementation (Wilkins *et al.*, 1989). White clover in the diet of beef cattle is also associated with an improved ratio of protein: fat in the carcases of beef cattle (Beever and Thorp, 1996).

At present there is relatively little reliance on white clover in the British dairy sector except on organic farms. This is in marked contrast to the situation in New Zealand where all pastoral agriculture is based almost entirely on grass/white clover swards. The adoption of white clover-based systems is a challenging area for UK dairy farmers to improve their efficiency. White clover can contribute to improved production on dairy farms, both at grazing and from silage. One study, in Ireland, compared output from spring-calving cows on N-fertilised grass (360 kg/ha) with grass/white clover. Milk production from the clover-based system was 2800 litres/cow at a stocking rate of 2.1 cows/ha, but greatest output/ha was obtained on the N-fertilised system at a higher stocking rate (Ryan, 1989). Increasing the amount of white clover in the diet of grazing cows has shown significant responses in milk yield (low clover 23.1 kg/day and high clover 25.9 kg/day) and also of milk protein and milk fat (Wilkins *et al.*, 1994).

Realising the potential of white clover

White clover requires reasonable levels of soil fertility for successful establishment and to maintain productivity. Soil pH of >5.5 and adequate soil P and K indices (or application of K P fertilisers in the seedbed) are usually recommended (Sheldrick *et al.*, 1987). Establishment, whether by complete reseeding or by drilling white clover, e.g. with a Hunter rotary strip seeder into an existing grass sward, also requires attention to detail (Table 6.2). Replacement of potassium on swards that are mown is needed to prevent its depletion, especially on light textured soils. In a 3-year cutting trial on a clay soil at North Wyke the mean annual DM harvested was 3.6 t/ha and 8.0 t/ha for nil fertiliser and lime + PK treatments, respectively, and the proportion of white clover was greatly reduced on the nil fertiliser treatment (Hopkins and Gilbey, 1995). The use of fertiliser N on grass white/clover swards is best avoided, or at least restricted to small tactical applications to increase herbage growth in early spring (Morrison *et al.*, 1983).

The most widely used white clover variety in Britain has been Grasslands Huia. Rhodes and Ortega (1996) considered that reliance on this variety, together with inappropriate use of N fertiliser, has mitigated against the realization of optimum clover content. Advances in white clover breeding have resulted in a 25% increase in agronomic performance since white clover breeding began in the 1920s (Caradus, 1993). In recent years a number of UK-bred varieties have been released. These offer advantages which justify the higher seed costs, particularly in terms of winter survival and spring growth as exemplified by AberCrest and AberHerald. Although leaf size is no longer a satisfactory basis for classifying varieties for use and persistency, small leaved types (e.g. S184 and Gwenda) in a mixture with a medium sized variety (e.g. Menna) are appropriate for intensive sheep grazing. Under

Table 6.2   Key guidelines for successful establishment and management of grass/white clover swards

Preparation and sowing

Conventional reseeding

1. Control perennial weeds before sowing.
2. Ensure soil pH is at least 5.5
3. Ensure adequate soil nutrients (P and K at MAFF index 2).
4. Clover seed rate of 3 to 4 kg/ha with compatible companion grass.
5. Choose varieties appropriate for intended use.
6. On sites with no previous white clover (some ex-arable, peaty and hill soils) use seed inoculated with *Rhizobium*.
7. Sow in spring or late summer.
8. Sow shallow (< 1cm) e.g. broadcast and roll.

Surface sowing

Above points 1 to 7, plus:

9. Avoid very heavy clay or stony sites.
10. Avoid sowing in very dry or excessively wet periods.
11. Sow into an open sward; closely graze or mow the sward first.

Subsequent management

1. Use only clover-safe herbicides, or avoid completely.
2. Avoid fertiliser N, or use only strategically (e.g. 50 kg/ha).
3. Avoid continuous severe grazing.
4. Provide periods for clover to recover, e.g. for a silage cut, but avoid excessive herbage growth.

less intensive cattle grazing, with integrated silage cutting, a mixture of medium- and large-leaved varieties is more appropriate. Once established, white clover seedlings spread by stolon growth to fill gaps in the sward, and a large stolon network can develop from relatively few plants. A sward in which white clover comprises about 30% of the total annual herbage yield is often recommended as optimal, though the proportion may vary from 5% to 50% at different times of year, and also vary between years. Intrinsic oscillations affect the relative proportions of grass and white clover over a 3 to 4 year cycle. These oscillations result from N-fixation, from the clover, which becomes available to its competitor grass species, and so benefits their production. In practice this means that year-to-year variation in clover, which equates with the farmer's perception of uncertainty or unreliability, is inevitable (Schwinning and Parsons, 1996).

Loss of white clover may result from winter kill, pests such as Sitona weevil and slugs (Clements, 1997), diseases (Thomas, 1997) and inappropriate management. Choice of variety may affect susceptibility to pests and diseases (Murray, 1996) and management should aim to prevent excessive herbage growth, depletion of soil nutrients, poaching and excessively severe grazing.

Sward grazing height is an important management variable which can affect sward productivity and the proportion of clover. Under continuous sheep grazing the optimum production is achieved at 4 to 6cm sward surface height (Orr *et al.*, 1990). N cycling occurs rapidly under this management, even though the proportion of clover may be temporarily reduced. Higher sward heights enable the grass to head, which should be avoided. Cattle can be grazed at a higher sward height (6 to 8cm) though at both 9 cm and at 4.5 cm (sward heights that are higher and lower than recommended) white clover content and sward production are reduced.

The possibility of bloat is of concern especially in relation to cows grazing clover-rich swards. Risks can be reduced by operating set-stocking rather than rotational grazing, by ensuring cattle are not allowed periods to get hungry (e.g. at milking), and ensuring that they are not suddenly introduced or allowed to break into lush clover-rich swards. The presence of some weedy species (e.g. docks) which contain condensed tannins has been shown to reduce or prevent bloat in feeding trials (Waghorn and Jones, 1989).

White clover is generally regarded as a grazing legume, but in association with suitable grasses it can produce good quality crops of silage, or even hay, which are sustainable over many years. For silage, wilting and the use of additives are usually recommended to ensure a good fermentation. White clover's ability to maintain digestibility also offers some flexibility in mowing dates. Swards of perennial ryegrass/white clover are well suited to integrated cutting and grazing, and imposing a silage cut as a break from intensive sheep grazing can increase the proportion of white clover in the sward.

The economic potential of white clover

The benefits of white clover, in terms of N fixation and feeding value, confer significant financial gains on livestock farmers who switch from conventional N-fertilised grass to systems based on grass/white clover. This is supported by a number of economic studies which show that, compared with systems using about 200 kg N/ha, grass/white clover swards can improve profits per hectare (Doyle and Bevan, 1996). The economic benefits of grass/clover appear greater for beef rearing and lamb production, where generally more extensive grazing systems are practised. The financial advantages disappear when comparisons are made with heavily stocked swards receiving 300 to 400 kg N/ha. However, when assessments are made on a per-animal basis, the lower potential carrying capacity of grass/white clover is excluded from the comparison, and clover-based systems show an appreciable financial advantage. Further evidence to support these findings comes from the field trials at Crichton Royal, Scotland (Bax and Schills, 1993) and Johnstown Castle, Ireland (Ryan, 1988).

Results from these studies show that systems based on grass/white clover can produce a gross margin per hectare higher than that achievable from a grass sward receiving 200 kg N/ha. Relatively few grassland farmers in Britain use fertiliser N at amounts in excess of this, particularly on non-dairy farms, and thus a switch from fertiliser N-based systems can be achieved without reducing stocking rates. Doyle has considered how, under the most favourable scenarios, the widespread adoption of white clover-based swards could increase dairy farming incomes by £20 to 40 per cow, and livestock farming by £20 to 30 per beef animal, or £10 to 15 per fat lamb (Hopkins *et al.*, 1994). These total benefits to UK livestock producers could exceed £300 million per year.

Given the advantages that exist in favour of grass/white clover swards, the progress made in white clover breeding and the understanding of its agronomy and management, it is paradoxical that white clover's role in British grassland is still vastly below its potential. Many technical constraints have been reduced, though systems based on white clover are often seen as carrying risk, particularly in terms of annual variations, and this may be a deterrent to their adoption (Doyle *et al.*, 1987). But it is often forgotten that the yield of N-fertilised grass is also highly variable between years. A further problem is that herbage production from grass/white clover may not meet peak demands in spring, and although management options exist to help overcome this problem it is still a deterrent for the farmer familiar with the simplicity of N-fertilised spring grass. For many farmers the real problem is a lack of experience of using grass/clover swards.

In terms of livestock production, UK agriculture enjoys a competitive advantage over most European countries. The UK has a good climate for pasture production, a farm structure that ensures low labour costs, and technical advantages in terms of research and development support for farmers. It is paramount that these advantages are maintained. In the long term, economic necessity to reduce production costs to meet the more open market of lower world prices will force many farmers to adopt more sustainable systems, and increased reliance on white clover will be one of the main means of achieving this within the ruminant production sectors.

References

BAX J.A. and SCHILLS R.L.M. (1993) Animal responses to white clover. In: *White clover in Europe - state of the art. REUR Technical Series 29.* Rome: FAO, pp 7-16.

BEEVER D.E. and THORP C. (1996) Advances in the understanding of factors influencing the nutritive value of legumes. In: Younie D. (ed.) *Legumes in Sustainable Farming Systems. Occasional Symposium no.30, British Grassland Society*, pp 194-207.

CARADUS J.R. (1993) Progress in white clover agronomic performance through breeding. *Proceedings XVII International Grassland Congress*, pp.396-397.

CHALMERS A.G., DYER C.J., LEECH P.K. and ELSMERE J.I. (1992) *Survey of Fertilizer Practice.* ADAS/FMA.

CLARK H. (1988) Beef and sheep output from grass/white clover swards. In: *The Grassland Debate: White Clover versus Applied Nitrogen. Proceedings RASE/ADAS Conference*, pp.12-16.

CLEMENTS R.O. (1997) Pests of grass and forage. In: *Seeds of Progress.* Proceedings BGS/BSPB/NIAB/SAC Conference. British Grassland Society.

COWLING D.W. (1982) Biological nitrogen fixation and grassland production in the United Kingdom. *Philosophical Transactions of the Royal Society of London, B.* 296, 397-404.

DAVIES D.A. and MUNRO J.M.M. (1988) Assessment of grass/clover pastures for lowland and upland lamb production. *Proceedings of 12th General Meeting of European Grassland Federation*, pp. 164-167.

DOYLE C.J. and BEVAN K. (1996) Economic effects of legume based grassland systems. In: Younie D (ed.) *op.cit.*, pp.247-256.

DOYLE C.J., MORRISON J. and PEEL S. (1987) Prospects for grass-clover swards in beef production systems: a computer simulation of the practical and economic implications. *Agricultural Systems,* **24**, 119-148.

FUSSEL G.E. (1964) The grasses and grassland cultivation of Britain. *Journal of the British Grassland Society,* **19**, 49-54.

GIBB M.J. and TREACHER T.T. (1983) The performance of lactating ewes offered diets containing different proportions of fresh perennial ryegrass and white clover. *Animal Production,* **37**, 433-440.

GIBB M.J. and TREACHER, T.T. (1984) The performance of weaned lambs offered diets containing different proportions of fresh perennial ryegrass and white clover. *Animal Production,* **39**, 412-420.

HOPKINS A., WAINWWRIGHT J., MURRAY P.J., BOWLING P.J. and WEBB M. (1988) 1986 Survey of upland grassland in England and Wales changes in age structure and botanical composition since 1970-72 in relation to grassland management and physical features. *Grass and Forage Science,* **43**, 185-198.

HOPKINS A., DAVIES D.A. and DOYLE C.J. (1994) Clover and other grazed legumes in UK pasture land. IGER Technical Review 1, 61pp.

HOPKINS A., MURRAY P.J., BOWLING P.J., ROOK A.J. and JOHNSON J. (1995) Productivity and nitrogen uptake of ageing and newly sown swards of perennial ryegrass (*Lolium perenne* L.) at different sites and with different fertilizer treatments. *European Journal of Agronomy,* **4**, 65-75.

HOPKINS A. And GILBEY J. (1995) An evaluation of the performance of two white clover varieties and a resident white clover on an acid, permanent grassland clay soil. *Plant Varieties and Seeds,* **8**, 67-72.

MORRISON J., DEHENY H.L. and CHAPMAN P.F. (1983) Possibilities for the strategic use of fertilizer N on white clover/grass swards. In: Corral A.J. (ed.) *Efficient Grassland Farming. Occasional Symposium no. 14, British Grassland Society,* pp. 227-231.

MOSELY G. and JONES J.R. (1994) The physical digestion of perennial ryegrass (*Lolium perenne*) and white clover (*Trifolium repens*) in the foregut of sheep. *British Journal of Nutrition,* **52**, 381-390.

MURRAY P.J. (1996) Evaluation of a range of varieties of white clover for resistance to feeding by weevils of the genus Sitona. *Plant Varieties and Seeds,* **9**, 9-14.

NEWBOULD P. (1982) Biological nitrogen fixation in upland and marginal areas of the UK. *Philosophical Transactions of the Royal Society of London, B.* 296, 405-417.

NEWTON J.E. and DAVIES D.A. (1987) White clover and sheep production. In: Pollot G.E. (ed.) *Efficient Sheep Production from Grass. Occasional Symposium No. 21, British Grassland Society,* pp. 79-87.

ORR R.J., PARSONS A.J., PENNING P.D. and TREACHER T.T. (1990) Sward composition, animal performance and potential production of grass/white clover swards continuously stocked with sheep. *Grass and Forage Science*, **45**, 325-336.

RHODES I. and ORTEGA F. (1996) Progress in forage legume breeding. In: Younie D. (ed.) *op.cit.*, pp.62-71.

RYAN M. (1988) Irish studies on milk production from grass/white clover swards. *The Grassland Debate: White clover Versus Applied Nitrogen*, (Royal Agricultural Society of England), Stoneleigh, 19 October 1988.

RYAN M. (1989) Development of a legume-based dairy system. *Developments in Plant and Soil Science*, **37** 159-167.

SCHWINNING S. And PARSONS A.J. (1996) Interactions between grasses and legumes: understanding variability in species composition. In: Younie E. (ed.) *op.cit.*, pp. 153-163.

SHELDRICK R., THOMSON D. And NEWMAN G. (1987) *Legumes for Meat and Milk*. Chalcombe Publications.

THOMAS J. (1997) Plant diseases. In: *Seeds of Progress*. Proceedings BGS/BSPB/NIAB/SAC Conference. British Grassland Society.

THOMSON D.J. (1984) The nutritive value of white clover. In: Thomson D.J. (ed.) *Forage Legumes. Occasional Symposium No. 16, British Grassland Society*, pp.78-92.

ULYATT M.J., LANCASHIRE J.A. and JONES W.T. (1977) The nutritive value of legumes. *Proceedings of the New Zealand Grassland Association*, **38**, 107-118.

WAGHORN G.C. and JONES W.T. (1989) Bloat in cattle. 46. Potential of dock (*Rumex obtusifolius*) as an antibloat agent for cattle. *New Zealand Journal of Agricultural Research*, **32**, 227-235.

WILKINS R.J., PEEL S., YARROW N.H., JOHNSON R.H. and FISHER A. (1989) Beef production based on white clover: effects of grazing management, concentrate supplementation and breed type. *Proceedings, 16th International Grassland Congress, Nice, 1989*, pp. 1229-1230.

WILKINS R.J., GIBB M.J., HUCKLE C.A. and CLEMENTS A.J. (1994) Effects of supplementation on production by spring-calving dairy cows grazing swards of differing clover content. *Grass and Forage Science*, **49** 465-475.

Chapter 7

The Potential of Red Clover in Organic Farming

O. Dowding

Shepton Farms Ltd, Hill Farm House, Shepton Montague, Wincanton, Somerset BA9 8JW

Summary

Red clover is a grossly underrated crop, which could benefit a huge number of livestock farmers in the UK, and even some solely arable farmers. It is particularly suited to the larger organic farm, or to one where there is off-lying land, because of its ability to fix large quantities of nitrogen and to produce high yields of high quality forage for either zero-grazing or silage making, and, on those farms that keep sheep, for fattening lambs in a way that few other crops are capable.

Introduction

I will briefly outline my own farm set up and hopefully illustrate why red clover is so valuable. The land area we farm extends to a 400 hectares, of which approximately one-third is tenanted. The centrepiece of the farm is the dairy unit where we have 290 cows at present, and for which we are currently carrying 240 youngstock, some of which will be sold as down-calving heifers. The farm began conversion to organic status in 1989 and completed the task in January 1993. We have been selling organic milk for most of the period since then. The demand for the product is hopelessly in excess of supply, and I have every confidence in recommending organic conversion to any farmer with some livestock and some cropping, or to one with a purely dairy enterprise. In the next milk quota year we will be receiving 29.5 pence per litre for our milk. My betting is that there will be few conventional dairy receiving a milk price rise this year, and that most will be receiving some form of reduced income, through either quality control costs or simple downwards price pressure. It is also worth noting that our milk contract is of a so-called 'white water' nature. If we produce 3.7% butterfat and 3.2% protein on a tanker-load adjusted basis, with TBC and cell-counts in the normal bandings, then our milk price is guaranteed.

For those of you with half a mind to the future, and who may already be growing clover successfully on the farm, the potential for conversion to organic production should be seriously considered seriously. There is now: a Conversion Scheme from MAFF, paying money to the converter; an assured premium for milk supplied to the Organic Milk Suppliers Co-Operative; and some free advice in the early stages of conversion. Putting all this together, and considering the welter of demand from consumers, would it not be sensible if more farmers voluntarily made the move to supply what is wanted rather than struggling to supply what is not so much in demand and for which the price is being squeezed downwards?

With the livestock on the farm producing a ready source of dung, from the covered yards and the lagoon, we are able to grow over 400 acres of arable crops in any one year. The layout of the farm does not allow us to take grazing cattle to every corner of it; and yet organically one can only cash crop each field a maximum of three times in any one rotation. The remaining period must be used for fertility building through the use of grass/clover leys. It is in this phase that we return the fertility to the soil, via the dung.

Establishing red clover

In order that the more distant fields have a fertility building phase we introduced red clover early in the organic conversion process. At the time I was unsure of a grass-seed mixture that would be suitable so I contacted Mole Valley Farmers and we formulated a mixture comprising 20 kg Merlinda Italian rye-grass and 4 kg Marcom red clover per hectare. Apart from a recent switch to Merviot red clover which provides us with better resistance against eelworm, we have stayed with the same mixture for the last six years, although we are now changing the ryegrass component. My preferred establishment is to undersow the ley in the spring. We do this by using a cover crop of peas. This may not be everybody's choice of cover crop, and it would not be mine in an ideal world, but one cannot ignore the potential to reap an Arable Area Payment!

We apply approximately 25 t/ha of FYM or slurry per hectare in the spring before reseeding. The reseed follows the two or three years of arable crops. The field is then ploughed, probably in February or March. It is ring-rolled shortly before being power-harrowed in late March or early April, according to the fortunes of the season, before drilling the peas. We ring-roll again; drill the grass/clover seed in one or two directions, depending on whether it is red or white clover; and then flat-roll. It is then a question of shutting the field gate and waiting until early July to take a cut of silage, which in most seasons ought to approach a yield of 20 to 22 t fresh weight/hectare. Last year saw some yields much higher than this, at a minimum of 35% DM. We have had high yields and low yields, and they are usually related to the timeliness of drilling and the dryness at that time.

The risks of lodging are relatively minor given that one is taking a silage crop and not waiting to harvest the peas as a mature grain crop. Under the terms of the Arable Aid Payments we have to wait until the peas have flowered before we cut. In practice of course we wait until the peas have formed inside the pod and have reasonable hardness.

We have experienced sowing red clover leys in the autumn and they have been more successfully established at that time of year than white clover leys. The rainfall in the autumn is very, very uncertain and in recent years it seems to have become more so. However, in August 1996 we sowed a red clover ley as an autumn reseed following set-aside, and took a cut of some 15 t/ha in October and had a mighty crop of grass for the sheep to graze in December.

For those insistent on regularly sowing in the autumn, one just has to abide by the normal good husbandry guidelines of sowing early and making sure that you have a good, level and well-rolled seedbed.

Threats to red clover

I will briefly mention threats to crop establishment. I know of only one, very wet, farm on low-lying land where they have had slug problems with their clover, but I think that is particular with the farm rather than the crop. My experience with our soils, which range from clay through to limestone brash, is that slugs are a grossly overrated problem. We have not found any crop loss due to slugs, although establishment of white clover, after a very wet period in May, was not as good as it should have been. I think red clover is more vigorous and able to grow away from attack better and quicker. We observe in general that with organic methods, the balance between predator and prey is better maintained, and exists across the whole field. We do not have the same paranoia about rooks as we did at the beginning of organic conversion, when they used to cause a certain amount of problem on emerging cereal crops which are grown with untreated seed and which do not have a bitter taste to the leaves that conventionally treated and dressed seed would appear to have.

We are quite pleased to see rooks on the farm as we know that they are eating slugs and other such delicacies. We are also aware that when we plough the fields, we see a tremendous swarm of seagulls and rooks following the plough. A contractor who ploughs here has often commented that the soil is easier to plough (through better structure) and that he sees far more birds following that he does on many other farms. This to me is an indicator of the number of earthworms and other invertebrates in the soil which act as a tasty snack for these birds.

Soil fertility

The conventional farmer, in using his slurry which acidifies the soil, does not always consider the impact it has upon the humble earthworm, nor the good that this little invertebrate can do to his soil. Earthworms leave behind them 5 times the nitrogen, 7 times the phosphate and 11 times the potash as available mineral compared to the availability of these elements from the soil before it ingest it. To have these sort of assistants working for you is excellent, but you will not find them advertising in the local Job Centre. You have to nurture their existence and care for them in the same way that you care for your cows, and they will then turn round and care for you. How many of you have looked for earthworm casts on your land and assessed what might be about, or given it a second thought in recent years?

Whilst on this theme it is worth commenting that the nitrogen-fixation by clover can reach up to 250 kg N/ha and that this is available to succeeding crops. It is not the same as 250 kg N/ha coming out of plastic bags which is available immediately and if not utilised is usually lost to the watercourses or the air. Trials have repeatedly shown that the nitrogen release from ploughed up clover swards is a gradual affair and that the risk of pollution of rivers and streams by leached nitrates is considerably reduced compared to that from conventionally fertilised fields where similar quantities of available N are applied to the soil as that available from the clover plant itself.

Most of our soils are in a reasonable state for phosphate and potash, although some have indices of 1 and occasionally 0. Despise the fact that lower indices presumably depress production, I have a feeling that when the natural balance of the soil is accepted, the yield derived under an organic regime from low index soil is greater, in relative terms, than if one were trying to produce with fertiliser, where the low index has a greater yield-limiting influence. To correct phosphate deficiencies we are only allowed to use rock phosphate and highland slag. There is nothing that we are readily allowed to use in the potash line, although the highland slag has some benefit here as well.

All our manure is returned to the red clover swards whilst they are in that phase of the rotation. If we have a suitable period, such as we did this year, we tend to go against the Soil Association guidelines and spread the muck whilst the ground is dry in the middle of the winter. If it is wet then we will hold off and apply it after we have taken the first cut of silage. Whichever way one does it, the muck needs to be well-rotted and not lumpy, and applied when there is the minimum amount of foliage growing, so that the muck is not lifted up into the cutting zone. We sometimes run the Einbok harrow comb (12m wide) over it.

Application rates of farmyard manure are 25 to 40 t fresh weight/hectare depending on soil analysis and crop offtake. Whilst it may be thought to be bad practice to be applying dung after first cut with a second crop in prospect some 8 weeks later because of the risk of grass contamination by the dung, the actual results do not support the theory. Experience shows that the 7 or 8 week period between cuts, the warm soil and the fact that the dung has gone on close to the soil, in as finely a spread form as possible, means that the earthworm activity is excellent and the dung is incorporated into the soil very quickly. For those who have not done so, I suggest that you take two flower pots filled with soil; into the first one put some earthworms and onto both of them chop some green leaves. See how quickly the leaves disappear from the one with the earthworms in, and how incredibly long the leaves take to rot down on the pot with no earthworms.

Utilising red clover

The value of red clover is extremely well-demonstrated in years of drought where its deep roots forage for water which is not as freely available to shallow-rooting white clovers, although even they do reasonably well. For those who have never had a red clover ley and seen it ploughed out, you would be amazed to see the roots springing back out of the 6 inch furrow slice. They are the size of very large dandelion roots or a small dock roots and as you can imagine the organic matter released from their decay is of tremendous value to soil quality and structure.

The same deep and active root system is good at drawing water from the sub-soil of the field in times of water shortage and the last two years (1995 and 1996) have given us ample experience too prove the point. We have had some excellent red clover for zero grazing in early August in both the dry years, and in many ways it has been salvation for the dairy herd.

In terms of bloat, I would be unwilling to recommend that anyone should direct-graze red clover, although I know that some have done so. In general it is a crop for ensiling or zero-grazing and not for grazing. You may get away with it, as I have done in dry times, so long as the animals graze after and before the dew leaves and returns to the sward. Sheep can benefit enormously from red clover and fattening lambs thrive on it.

Our silage making technique is no different to that of anyone else. We mow; we sometimes spread, depending on the bulk of the sward and the weather pattern; we row up and we ensile with a precision chop forage harvester. I have been a great fan of Live System Additive on red clover silage but like many I am starting to fine tune our additive requirements. My favoured view for next season is to have some Live System on stand-by but only to use it if the weather conditions look catchy. If we have a dry spell we should be able to ensile at over 30% dry matter and avoid the need for additive altogether. The higher DM will also have a beneficial effect on forage intakes, and roll through into milk produced from forages.

This leads on to the next advantage of red clover and white clover: flexible timing of silage-making. Whereas those people who find it irresistible to grow straight Italian ryegrass swards will get a large first cut of silage they will be obliged to do so before a certain date unless they want to see the digestibility (D-value) of the sward deteriorate at an alarming rate. One of the undoubted advantages of clover is that it maintains that value for considerably longer than the ryegrass equivalent. My experience is that it also has a suppressant effect on the heading of the companion ryegrass, therefore we retain the D-value in the overall sward. We can choose our cutting date within a reasonably extended window of opportunity and pick a dry slot for silage making which we do ourselves.

The same advantage applies to second and third cut silage. It has the benefit of not having to be cut more than every 7 to 8 weeks, so three cuts in a season is acceptable. The retention of the quality in three big cuts is important.

Yield is of paramount importance to all farmers, and my estimate is that we achieving between 12 and 13 t of dry matter ensiled per hectare from 3 cuts. There is, in addition, an amount of sheep grazing to be had in late autumn. Where we are cutting in the first sowing year with a spring reseed, we would expect a yield of 7 to 9 t DM/ha in the first cut of arable silage together with 2.5 to 4 t DM/ha from the second cut in late September.

In terms of feeding I am inclined to believe, because of its relatively stalky nature, red clover almost takes the role of second forage within the silage ration in the winter. Naturally it does not have a grain, but the intense number of flowers that are ensiled might go some way towards making up the grain part of the whole-crop cereal silage. We currently ensile all cuts together, so it is difficult to identify different bands of silage and to know where the red clover ends up.

Conclusions

Red clover is a crop overflowing with potential, underrated by nearly everybody and offering everyone the chance to get off the chemical treadmill, unless you are addicted to the smell of ammonium nitrate fertilisers and urea and that of the chemicals which some still seem to find necessary to use in order to grow crops. I have to tell you that, in growing the succeeding crops of wheat, we have **not** found chemicals to be necessary, the bugs have **not** eaten the crops, the diseases have **not** pinched the grain, the pests have **not** destroyed the quality of the sample, the specific weights **have** been of the right standard and the resulting organic grain yield of 5.3 t/ha sold in 1996 at considerably more than £200/t is an added bonus to a red clover crop which is brimming over with potential for most farms. Why do you feel the need to plaster one field with excessive amounts of slurry in order to grow one maize crop per year? In doing so you are killing the earthworms and pitching all your eggs in one basket labelled 'maize', and hoping that the black nightshade and other weeds do not outstrip your ability to control them with chemicals. If you are getting 4500 litres from forage and using maize maybe you are doing it well, but for many the answer is that they are not and red clover would provide a much better alternative.

Do not forget the **organic option** because this will be the way to regain control of your farming business from those who currently siphon money out of it in order to provide them with an income from their products which they sell to you, or your produce which they market for you.

Chapter 8

Sainfoin:
The not quite forgotten Legume

R. Hill

Cotswold Grass Seeds, The Barn Business Centre,
Great Rissington, Cheltenham, Gloucestershire GL54 2LH

Summary

Sainfoin is a non-bloating legume, of similar size to lucerne, which grows best on dry soils. The crop should be established in spring or early summer. One of the reasons for the decline in the popularity of sainfoin has been the dominance of autumn-sown arable crops in the UK. Yields are typically about 70% of lucerne. The protein in sainfoin is protected by tannins from degradation in the rumen, and as a result absorption of protein in the small intestine is increased compared to other forages. There is a lack of research into sainfoin and there is considerable potential for its yield to be increased by plant breeding or by genetic engineering.

Introduction

Cotswold Grass Seeds came into sainfoin as a legacy from the seed firm Townsends of Stroud only 12 miles from here. For many years they were the chief suppliers of sainfoin both as straight seed in the pod and also as milled seed in mixtures with grasses and clovers. Their directors, Jimmy Walwin and the late Douglas Dash were enthusiasts and in the late 1950s they were still selling 150 tonnes or more of seed per year, enough to plant 5 or 6 thousand acres.

The history of the crop is an interesting one. A book which I found in the library of the Royal Agricultural College published in 1652 refers to a sack of sainfoin seed coming on a ship from Calais together with 4 sorts of lucerne. Of the two, it was sainfoin which became popular and during the 18th and 19th centuries several writers gave a description of how to grow it. From these accounts it is clear that the crop was widely appreciated and understood. Arthur Young said in his General View of the Agriculture of Oxfordshire in 1813, "The merit of Oxfordshire farming is more conspicuous on account of sainfoin on all soils that are proper for it". By the 1950s it was still described by a Cotswold farmer as, "one of the best cogs in the wheels of the ley system".

Seed of sainfoin, like that of all the larger legumes, has suffered a dramatic drop in sales and now there are only a few tonnes sold each year. Jimmy Walwin is still an enthusiast and has been helpful in keeping the seed stocks of Cotswold Common from dying out. I would like to pay tribute to this remarkable seedsman with over 70 years' experience in the field.

Sainfoin, apart from its agricultural value, is an attractive plant and should be liked by environmentalists. The rules for Environmentally-Sensitive Areas (ESAs) do not, however, allow its use. One of our customers had to plough up 50 acres of newly established sainfoin before he could get an ESA agreement.

The plant is similar in size to lucerne but belongs to the genus *Onobrychis*. There are several types of sainfoin and some are classified as *Hedysarum* although appearing to be similar.

Producing and utilising sainfoin

Some technical aspects of producing and utilising sainfoin are summarised in Table 8.1. Dry and warm soils, typically thin chalk or limestone brash soils, suit sainfoin and it will grow well on those stony fields which are a speciality in the Cotswolds. This is not to say it will not grow on any well drained soil with a pH of around 6.0. Like lucerne, it is a deep rooting plant but it is considered the more drought resistant and more winter hardy, explaining its use in Canada and Russia.

The seed is quite different to that of lucerne, being contained in a pod, and much larger. Like lucerne, it needs to be sown in the spring or early summer. One of the reasons for the decline of these legumes was probably the dominance of autumn cereal planting, a trend which started in the 1960s, and which now accounts for about 90% of all cereal crops on arable farms. Establishment of either sainfoin or lucerne after say winter barley, (i.e. late July/August), is risky as the seedlings do not have time to establish before winter. More spring planting of cereals should allow better opportunities for establishing both crops, perhaps by undersowing maize.

Table 8.1   Technical aspects of sainfoin (Source: IGER)

Sowing the crop

Seed rate:	25 kg per acre = 82 kg per hectare
Depth of sowing:	1 to 2 cm
Plant density required:	70 to 150 plants per m^2 at establishment
	50 to 60 plants per m^2 at end of first season
Companion grasses:	Meadow fescue 4 to 5 kg per hectare (preferred)
	Timothy 1 to 2 kg per hectare
	White clover 0.5 to1 kg per hectare

Livestock performance

Liveweight gain (g/day) of lambs:

Perennial ryegrass:	193
Lucerne:	257
Sainfoin:	288

Inoculation of seed has not been considered necessary in the UK but there is a culture available in Canada.

Cultivars - we have no bred strains of sainfoin whereas there are over 80 for lucerne. A new variety, Nova, can be obtained from Canada and another, Emir, was produced by Tibor Emetz but this has not been multiplied.

Fertiliser and spraying requirements are similar to those for lucerne. Also, the arguments for and against using a companion grass are the same.

Yield - this was shown at the Institute of Grassland and Environmental Research (IGER), Hurley, to be 70% of lucerne. The first cut can produce 5 tonnes DM/hectare and annual production can be expected to be in the region of 7 to 12 tonnes. Canadian experience using the cultivar Nova averaged 11 tonnes in 3 cuts over 3 years. Thus it is lower yielding than lucerne although it may perform better in a dry summer.

It is when animal production is considered that sainfoin comes into its own. Together with birdsfoot trefoil (*Lotus*), sainfoin has the distinction of being a non-bloating legume due to the presence of tannins in the leaves. The high protein content, 15 to 25% of the dry matter, is protected by the tannins in the rumen. This leads to much better absorption of protein in the lower gut. Work at IGER showed a 50% increase in protein absorbed compared with lucerne. This large increase helps to explain the very high liveweight gains obtained at Hurley with lambs fed on sainfoin.

In common with other legumes, the cell wall content is low and decline in digestibility is slower than for grass as the plants mature. Voluntary feed intake is highest with sainfoin due to its palatability both as hay, silage or grazing.

Tannins in addition to aiding the digestion of proteins also improve the intake of energy (ME) and it has been shown that lower carcass fat levels may also be achieved - a very important objective of our sheep industry. This area needs further research.

We are now the New Zealand of Europe, exporting and producing more sheepmeat than any other EU country. This important legume could make a contribution to the economics of lamb production in the UK. I suspect that the popularity of sainfoin by generations of stock farmers was mainly due to the very high liveweight gains and quality of meat achieved.

Responses from sainfoin are greatest when the animal has a high requirement of protein. Thus it should be fed mainly to young stock especially lambs, also calves both beef and dairy. For horses it has always been considered the Rolls-Royce of feeds and the hay is highly saleable. By re-establishing food intake after a period of ill-health (the "physic" property) it was renowned by farmers in the past.

The potential for milk production is not clear but I think that lucerne either zero grazed or as silage is the better route.

Conclusions

I have described the history of sainfoin, its decline to a very small acreage and compared it with lucerne. Although lower yielding, its special nutritional and non-bloating qualities distinguish it from lucerne as an excellent grazing species.

It remains for someone to improve the yield using plant breeding or genetic engineering techniques. Further work is also needed with regard to tannins and there is always the possibility of transferring these to other species. Sainfoin provides a fertile ground for researchers as not much work has been done on it.

In meeting the protein requirements of ruminant animals it is no exaggeration to state that sainfoin is the most efficient plant available for forage.

The last conference on sainfoin was at IGER, Hurley, in 1982 when its future was discussed. Since then nothing has happened. The question which I put to the conference is: do we allow this species to become like Cotswold sheep, a rare breed, or do we go forward with it in the future?

Chapter 9

Forage Maize and Whole-Crop Fodder Beet for Young Beef Cattle

D.G. Chapple, H.F. Grundy and M.H. Davies

ADAS Rosemaund, Preston Wynne, Hereford HR1 3PG

Summary

Forage maize and whole-crop fodder beet silages are alternatives to conserved grass. These crops have a high yield potential and require harvesting only once per season, but are low in protein.

An experiment conducted at ADAS Rosemaund investigated the performance of 4-month old bulls fed ad libitum on maize (M) or fodder beet (F) silages. Forage maize was harvested in early October at 30.2% dry matter. Fodder beet roots and tops were harvested in late September, mixed with a 34% crude protein absorbent and chopped barley straw at the clamp, to produce a 24.3% dry matter silage. Both silages were supplemented with 2.0 kg of a rolled barley/rapeseed meal supplement, with the rapeseed fed at three different proportions in the supplement; 0.4 (M40), 0.6 (M60) or 0.8 (M80) for the maize silage ration, and 0.2 (F20), 0.4 (F40) or 0.6 (F60) for the whole-crop fodder beet ration. The six treatment diets were each given to 15 Limousin x Friesian bulls (mean initial liveweight 164 kg) in three pen replicates of five animals for an experimental period of 120 days.

High rates of liveweight gain were achieved by bulls on both forages, with those on F rations being higher (P<0.05) than those on M rations (1.30 v 1.21 kg/day). However increasing the proportions of rapeseed meal in the supplement had no effect on growth rates on either ration. Liveweight gains (LWG) were 1.19, 1.24, 1.20, 1.28,

1.30 and 1.32 kg/day for M40, M60, M80, F20, F40 and F60 respectively Silage dry matter intakes were higher for bulls on M rations (3.90 v 3.57 kg DM/day), but food conversion efficiencies were better on the F rations (4.49 v 3.93 kg DM/kg LWG).

Introduction

Feed accounts for approximately two-thirds of the variable costs of beef production (Hardy and Meadowcroft, 1986). Forage-based diets are important in high output ruminant production systems as they are the cheapest source of energy and protein. In the UK, grass silage is currently the main conserved forage used in beef systems. Whole-crop fodder beet silage and forage maize silage are alternatives to conserved grass, having yield potentials of 20 and 15 tonnes of dry matter per hectare respectively (NIAB, 1990). These crops require only one harvesting operation, compared to three cuts of grass required to produce 11 tonnes of dry matter per hectare. However both forage maize and fodder beet are low in protein. Research at Rosemaund (Chapple *et. al.*, 1993) showed an increase in daily liveweight gain when whole-crop fodder beet silage was compared with grass silage.

The objective of this experiment was to compare whole-crop fodder beet silage with maize silage when fed with different levels of rapeseed meal to young beef cattle.

Materials and methods

The maize (cv. LG2080) was harvested at 30.2% dry matter (DM) on 8 October 1992 with an average yield of 13.2 tonnes DM per hectare. The whole crop fodder beet (cv. Kyros) was harvested on 29 September at 18.1 tonnes DM per hectare. At the silo, an absorbent (VitaSorb, Cowe Agriculture Ltd.) containing 34% crude protein (CP) and chopped barley straw, was incorporated with the chopped whole-crop fodder beet to give an overall DM content of 24.3% at ensilage.

The silages were fed to 90 Limousin x Friesian bulls from four to eight months of age. The young bulls were housed in a part-bedded/part-scraped finishing house throughout the 120-day experimental period. They were allocated to the treatment diets on 11 January 1993 and fed on forage with 2.0 kg fresh weight per head per day of a rolled barley/rapeseed meal supplement.

Treatments

1. Maize silage *ad libitum* + 1200 g barley + 800 g rapeseed (M40)
2. Maize silage *ad libitum* + 800 g barley + 1200 g rapeseed (M60)
3. Maize silage *ad libitum* + 400 g barley + 1600 g rapeseed (M80)
4. Fodder beet silage *ad libitum* + 1600 g barley + 400 g rapeseed (F20)
5. Fodder beet silage *ad libitum* + 1200 g barley + 800 g rapeseed (F40)
6. Fodder beet silage *ad libitum* + 800 g barley + 1200 g rapeseed (F60)

Three replicates of 5 bulls were allocated to each treatment giving 15 bulls per treatment.

Results

Both silages were well fermented (Table 9.1). The crude protein (CP) content of the fodder beet silage had been substantially boosted by the high CP absorbent. The six diets had overall CP contents (g/kg DM) of 146 (M40), 158 (M60), 170 (M80), 182 (F20), 194 (F40) and 209 (F60).

Table 9.1   Composition of feeds at feeding

	Maize silage	Fodder beet silage	Rapeseed meal	Barley
Dry matter (g/kg)	329	276	869	849
pH	3.7	3.7	-	-
Crude protein (g/kg DM)	94	163	387	129
Ammonia N (g/kg total N)	72	45	-	-
NCGD (g/kg DM)	701	630	-	-
Ash (g/kg DM)	44	172	-	-
Starch (g/kg DM)	155	26	-	-
Estimated ME (MJ/kg DM)	11.0	*	-	-

* No standard equation available

Bulls fed on maize silage averaged 1.21 kg per head per day liveweight gain compared with 1.30 kg per day for those fed on the fodder beet silage (p<0.05, Table 9.2). However, increasing the rate of protein supplementation did not affect the performance of bulls given either silage. The silage dry matter intakes were similar for bulls fed maize silage irrespective of level of protein supplementation (Table 9.2). Bulls fed on diet F40 ate significantly more silage than bulls fed F20 (P<0.05). Silage intakes were higher for animals fed on maize silage than for those given fodder beet silage (3.90 v 3.57 kg/day, P<0.05).

Table 9.2　　**Animal growth performance, food intake and food conversion efficiency**

	Maize silage			Fodder beet silage			
	M40	**M60**	**M80**	**F20**	**F40**	**F60**	**s.e.d**
Start weight (kg)	163	163	163	163	163	163	0.8
End weight (kg)	306	312	306	316	319	321	5.6
Liveweight gain (kg/head/day)	1.19	1.24	1.20	1.28	1.30	1.32	0.045
Silage DM intake (kg/head/day)	3.81	3.94	3.94	3.38	3.74	3.60	0.153
Total DM intake (kg/head/day)	5.52	5.66	5.67	5.07	5.45	5.32	0.153
Food conversion (FCE) (kg DM/kg gain)	4.48	4.41	4.58	3.83	4.05	3.90	0.093

Food conversion efficiencies were excellent on all treatments and were as good as or better than those expected on cereal beef systems. Bulls fed on diets F40 and F60 produced significantly better food conversion efficiencies (P<0.001) than those given diets M40 and M60. However, the whole-crop fodder beet silage was enhanced by a high protein absorbent at ensilage, and bulls given this silage had a higher overall protein intake than those fed on the diets based on maize silage.

Conclusions

1. The levels of protein supplementation evaluated in this experiment did not produce differential rates of live-weight gain for bulls fed whole-crop fodder beet silage or maize silage.

2. Bulls fed on whole-crop fodder beet silage had higher rates of live-weight gain than bulls fed maize silage.

3. Food conversion efficiency was improved for bulls fed whole-crop fodder beet silage compared to those given diets based on maize silage.

4. Young four month old calves will achieve high liveweight gains on either maize or fodder beet silage supplemented with 2.0 kg per head per day of a rolled barley/rapeseed meal supplement.

References

CHAPPLE, D.G., DAVIES, M.H. and GRUNDY, H.F. (1993) Whole-crop fodder beet silage for beef cattle. In: O'Kiely P., O'Connell M. and Murphy J. (eds.) *Silage Research.* Proceedings of the 10th International Conference on Silage Research, Dublin City University, pp 210-211.

HARDY, R. and MEADOWCROFT, S.C. (1986) *Indoor Beef Production.* Farming Press Ltd.

NIAB (1990). National Institute of Agricultural Botany. *Classified List of Fodder Crops, England and Wales.* NIAB, Cambridge.

Chapter 10

Big Bale Kale - The Scottish Perspective

J.E. Vipond[1], D.J. Allan[2], J. Veitch and D. Turner[3]

[1] *Genetics and Behavioural Sciences Department, Scottish Agricultural College, Bush Estate, Penicuik EH26 0QE*
[2] *Volac Ltd, 15 Abbots Way, Doonfoot, Ayr KA7 4EZ*
[3] *Oatridge College, Ecclesmachen, Broxburn EH52 6HH*

Summary

Around 2,000 ha of kale was grown in the UK in 1996 for ensilage in big bales wrapped in plastic. Weeds and baling problems occurred but were not insurmountable. Fermentation produced a stable product but dry matter content at 15% increased cost per tonne of ensiled material relative to grass silage. Results from both dairy and beef farms indicated the silage was very palatable to stock and gave good results.

Progress in the ensilage of kale

Big bale kale was pioneered by Devon dairy farmer Ron Patey leading to farmers throughout the UK experimenting with ensiled forage brassicas. Developments in Scotland are summarised in this paper. Scotland has historically been an area where forage brassicas are grown for dairy cattle on lowland farms and finishing lambs on hill and upland farms, however the acreage has fallen dramatically in recent years. Renewed interest can be attributed to increased demand for home grown conserved protein supplements following the BSE crisis. Also the recent problems of *E. coli* contamination of food in Scotland has made the cleanliness of stock presented to abattoirs more important. Thus there is interest in new systems of utilising forage brassicas by sheep that do not involve grazing and the associated contamination of fleeces.

Big bale kale grown in southern England fits well as a break crop (12 weeks) in the renewal of swards. It is sown after the first silage cut in May and harvested after 12 weeks as a catch crop; then the grass is sown. In Scotland the shorter growing season restricts the crop after kale to winter cereals or a spring-sown cereal. There is potential for aftermath growth after the first cut of kale. In Dumfries a crop sown on May 13th and harvested to a 12 cm stubble on July 31st yielded over 3 tonnes DM/ha of regrowth by late October. However crops harvested after September are unlikely to yield grazeable aftermath. A yield of 25 to 30 tonne silage/ha is typical at 15% dry matter costing £13 to 14/tonne of fresh weight.

Agronomy

Some weed problems have been encountered on farms, mainly fat hen. Pre-emergence treatment with Treflan is indicated or possibly post-emergence with Semeron. Where Treflan is used and the crop is heavily dunged following harvesting the residual effects of Treflan are no longer a problem.

Conservation

In some instances the mowers chopped up the kale stems because the conditioner spun too quickly. Both Lely and Taarrup mower conditioners have been found to be particularly good for big bale kale as the rotation speed of the conditioner can be quickly and easily slowed to about 300 rpm, resulting in less crop damage and less subsequent effluent production. Rape swathers have been used also but these reduce drying opportunity. Round bales generally weighed around a tonne and were netted then wrapped. Square bales weighing half a tonne have been made but the damage to stems increases the potential for effluent. The use of a biological additive to improve fermentation quality is recommended. Bales, when stored one high, produce little effluent.

Silage quality

The analysis of five Scottish big bale kale silages is shown in Table 10.1. Mean dry matter content has been around 15%, vs. 18.7% for England. The low DM of the crop compared with grass silage means that the cost per tonne of dry matter is high relative to grass silage (£90 vs. £60). This implies that we need to get better performance from the dry matter or the feed needs to be used more efficiently than grass silage if kale silage is going to be an economic proposition. Alternatively we need higher dry matter varieties of kale.

Table 10.1   Analysis of five Scottish big bale kale silages

	Mean	Range
DM (%)	153	13.3 to 16.1
ME (MJ/kg DM)	12	11.5 to 12.8
CP (g/kg DM)	180	160 to 212
Ash (g/kg DM)	150	99 to 219

Both the ME and crude protein (CP) were estimated by NIR using equations derived from grass silage and should be used with caution although the CP values were in good agreement with Kjeldahl values and the ME is considered to be realistic bearing in mind that ME values *in vivo* for fresh kale lie within the range of 11.0 to 12.7 MJ/kg DM. Ash content of 150 g/kg reflects the high mineral content of kale. Analysis indicates consistently high energy and protein content of silage dry matter.

Feeding of the crop

Dairy Cows

Most farmers are using the crop at a low level, typically 5 to 10 kg of silage fresh weight per cow per day, spreading out the crop over the whole of the winter feeding period. This offers savings in the purchase of protein supplements.

Table 10.2   Effect of big bale kale silage on lamb performance over 42 day finishing period

Kale silage: grass silage	Forage DM intake (kg)	Total DM intake (kg)	Initial liveweight (kg)	Daily gain (g)	Feed conversion ratio (TDMI/gain)	Cold carcass weight (kg)	Fat score	Carcase conformation	Killing-out percentage (%)
100:0	0.62	1.02	32.7	129	7.91	17.5	3.0	3.1	47.6
67:33	0.66	1.06	32.9	150	7.07	17.3	3.2	3.3	46.2
33:67	0.66	1.06	33.4	144	7.36	17.5	3.1	3.4	46.3
0:100	0.61	1.01	33.1	145	6.97	17.3	2.8	3.3	45.8
s.e.d	na	na	0.57	21	na	0.43	0.17	0.14	0.66
Level of significance	-	-	NS	NS	-	NS	NS	NS	*

Beef Cattle

On a Northumberland farm good performance and rapid finishing of beef cattle fed on 35 kg baled kale silage per day along with grass silage and concentrates has been reported with no antimetabolite problems. Interim results from Greenmount College in Co. Antrim, Northern Ireland, showed no improvement in performance by replacing 20% of grass silage with baled kale silage (19% DM) in beef cattle diets.

Sheep

In a lamb finishing trial at Oatridge College, pens of 20 Blackface wether lambs aged 9 months were offered diets of kale silage: grass silage in DM ratios of 100:0 (A) 67:33 (B) 33:67 (C) and 0:100 (D). Results for the six-week trial are shown in Table 10.2. Lambs with a proportion of kale silage in the diet did not perform better than lambs on grass silage alone. Intake may have been constrained by the low dry matter content of the kale silage. Killing out percentage increased with the proportion of kale silage in the ration.

The analysis of the kale and grass silages were respectively as follows, dry matter (%) 15.7 vs. 25.0, ME (MJ/kg DM) 11.5 vs. 11.1 and CP (g/kg DM) 175 vs. 141.

Conclusions

The uptake of big bale kale in Scotland has been fairly rapid, considerable numbers of farmers having the abilities and land suitable to grow the crop and the machinery and equipment for feeding the silage. A major problem of low dry matter has been identified in the silage, increasing the cost of storage and possibly reducing the feeding potential of the material. All classes of stock demonstrate unusually high preference for the material over grass silage in mixed diets. Results suggest that the material is useful for finishing animals and as a protein source for milk production. Many farmers who have grown the crop in 1996 have indicated they intend to increase the area sown to kale in 1997.

Chapter 11

Whole-Crop Barley and Oats Undersown with Italian Ryegrass/Red Clover as Big Bale Silage in an Organic System

E.L. Jones, J.E. Jones, R. Fychan, P. Bowling and R. Jones

Institute of Grassland and Environmental Research
Plas Gogerddan, Aberystwyth, Ceredigion SY23 3EB

Summary

One variety of barley (Hart), naked oats (Ripon) and husked oats (Aberglen) were undersown with Italian ryegrass/red clover. The cereal cover crops were harvested as big bale silage at the milk and dough stages of growth and aftermath grass growth measured. Cereal dry matter (DM) yield did not differ significantly at either milk or dough stages. Barley whole-crop silage was better fermented at both growth stages reflecting the higher DM and water soluble carbohydrates content of the crop. Aftermath yields were similar for cereals harvested at the milk stage but were higher after barley than oats when harvested at the dough stage. In the experiment described the barley variety was better suited to the organic system; other varieties of both cereals need to be assessed.

Introduction

The availability of sufficient high quality silage for winter feed and the establishment and maintenance of grass/clover pastures are vital to the success of organic dairy systems. It is known that whole-crop cereals can provide high yields of high quality silage (Lawes and Jones, 1971; Tetlow, 1990; Siefers *et al.*, 1996). Growing a cereal crop for silage as a cover crop for undersown grass/clover would allow the establishment phase to be utilised to provide additional winter feed, and it would appear to be potentially advantageous in an organic farm system. The chances of establishment failure are increased with undersowing but farm experience has shown that a satisfactory establishment can be achieved from sowing Italian ryegrass and red clover under cereals (IGER, 1996).

The present study compared the potential of whole-crop oat and barley, undersown with grass/clover, as conservation crops ensiled as big bale silage. A review (Bennett, 1988) concluded that further work on the value of whole-crop oats silage should be explored. The effects of undersowing on establishment and on the subsequent yields of the undersown grass/clover in an organically managed system were also examined.

Materials and methods

The experiment followed a perennial ryegrass dominant permanent pasture maintained under an organic regime for the past 5 years. Prior to ploughing, 50 tonnes of farmyard manure were applied per hectare in early spring. A field of 3.06 ha was ploughed in March 1996 and a seed-bed prepared incorporating 7 tonnes of lime per hectare. Two oat varieties, a naked variety (Ripon), a husked variety (Aberglen) and a barley variety (Hart) were undersown with an Italian ryegrass/red clover mixture in a randomised complete block design with three replicated plots each measuring 25 m x 80 m. Cereals were sown on 21 March at a seed rate of 130,220 and 240 kg/ha respectively, to give a target plant population of 300 plants/m^2. The pasture was sown 14 days later at a seed rate of 19.8 kg Italian ryegrass/ha and 12.3 kg red clover/ha. After each sowing the plots were rolled firmly using a smooth roller. Cereal seedling counts were made in three 1m lengths of drill per plot on 8 May. Light intercepted by the crops was measured by placing a small fibre optic meter centrally between the cereal rows. Four readings per plot were taken on 4 June and the intercepted light was calculated as a percentage of the light above the canopy.

Yields of DM were assessed at two stages of maturity - the milk and dough stages (8 and 17 July for barley and 17 and 31 July for oats) when the crops were harvested as big bale silage. Forage was cut with a disc mower and then picked up as round bales immediately using a Greenland round chopper-baler. Three bales were made for each replicate per treatment at each maturity date giving a total of 54 bales (3 bales x 3 vars x 3 reps x 2 maturity dates). The bales were weighed and sampled at harvest and again after a 90-day ensiling period using a 50 mm diameter motorised corer. After the silage harvest an aftermath cut was taken off the Italian ryegrass/red clover mixture on 19 September and DM production measured.

Results

Cereal establishment
Satisfactory establishment was achieved for all three cereals. Plant density counts were 347 plants/m^2 for the husked oat compared to 294 for the naked oat and 283 for the barley. The crops were relatively weed free, as the scratch bar of the undersowing drill was very effective in controlling young weed seedlings.

Photosynthetically-active radiation
The percentage of photosynthetically-active radiation passing through the canopy measured at Feekes growth stage 24 was higher for barley (7.3%) than for naked oat (5.8) and the husked oat (5.5) agreeing with visual assessment. The values recorded were, however, extremely variable and differences were not significant.

Cereal growth stages at harvest
The barley reached the late milk stage (growth stage 77) 109 days from sowing and the dough stage (86) in 118 days, both the oats reached the early milk (73) and the early dough (83) in 118 and 132 days respectively.

Forage production
Both naked and husked oats produced significantly more forage fresh weight than the barley when harvested at either the milk or dough stages (Table 11.1). The barley crops were significantly higher in DM content

at both harvests compared to the oats. Consequently, DM production did not differ significantly between the three cereals at either the milk or dough stages. DM production and DM content were higher for all three cereals when harvested at the dough compared to the milk stage.

Table 11.1   **Forage production (t/ha) and DM content (g/kg) of barley and oat crops harvested at the milk and dough stages**

	Fresh weight		Dry weight		DM content	
	Milk	*Dough*	*Milk*	*Dough*	*Milk*	*Dough*
Barley	34.7	33.4	8.64	9.85	249	295
Naked oats	44.9	45.7	9.04	10.23	201	224
Husked oats	49.0	47.7	9.36	10.57	191	222
S.E.	1.67	1.10	0.31	0.39	3.2	8.1
LSD (P<0.05)	4.13	2.72	NS	NS	8.0	20.1

NS = not significant

Table 11.2   **Chemical composition of cereal varieties harvested at the milk and dough stages of maturity**

	Nitrogen (g/kg DM)		WSC (g/kg DM)		DOMD (%)	
	Milk	*Dough*	*Milk*	*Dough*	*Milk*	*Dough*
Barley	14.3	14.3	177	109	60.0	59.9
Naked oats	15.7	13.1	90	63	54.1	52.4
Husked oats	15.0	13.6	82	55	53.2	52.7
S.E.	0.93	0.56	7.9	4.0	0.54	1.32
LSD (P<0.05)	NS	NS	19.6	9.9	1.34	3.28

Crop composition

The effect of stage of maturity at harvest of the three cereals on crop composition is shown in Table 11.2. The WSC content of barley in the early harvest was adequate to ensure a good fermentation (177g/kg DM), however, the barley in the later harvest and the two oat varieties at both harvest dates contained WSC levels below 110 g/kg DM. DOMD values were significantly higher for the barley than for the oat varieties.

Silage composition

Both early and late harvests of barley showed good fermentation characteristics with a pH value of less than 4.7, a DM of 253 to 304 g/kg and an ammonia-N content less than 60 g/kg of total N (Table 11.3). Preservation of whole-crop husked and naked oats was more variable with a higher ammonia-N content above 60 g/kg of total N, pH values exceeding 4.64 and a DM of 196 to 222 g/kg.

Table 11.3   **Composition of silages from cereal varieties harvested at the milk and dough stages of maturity**

	DM (g/kg)		pH		Ammonia-N (g/kg N)	
	Milk	*Dough*	*Milk*	*Dough*	*Milk*	*Dough*
Barley	252.9	303.6	4.29	4.63	54.5	46.7
Naked Oats	203.4	221.8	4.69	4.64	75.8	73.8
Husked Oats	196.7	214.9	4.67	4.98	67.3	90.7
SE	4.37	7.58	0.11	0.15	3.61	4.53
LSD (P<0.05)	10.84	18.79	0.27	NS	8.95	11.23

Aftermath growth

The later harvest suppressed the recovery growth of the undersown Italian ryegrass/red clover (Table 11.4). There were no significant differences in total DM production of the aftermath for the three cereal treatments if harvested at the milk stage. Aftermath production was highest following the barley and least after the husked oats. When cereals were cut at the dough stage grass/clover aftermath production was twice as high for the barley as for either of the oats. The proportion of clover in the grass/clover aftermath was higher for the barley treatments (29 to 31%) than for the oats (19 to 22%) but the difference was not significant.

Table 11.4   Aftermath grass/clover yields (t DM/ha) following cereal harvest at milk and dough stages

Cover crop	Milk stage	Dough stage
Barley	1.74	1.53
Naked oats	1.50	0.76
Husked oats	1.33	0.77
S.E.	0.28	0.16
LSD (P<0.05)	NS	0.34

Conclusions

The results show clearly that growing a cereal cover crop, harvested as baled silage, can provide a good source of winter feed in an organic system while successfully establishing an undersown grass/clover ley. The spring barley variety used in this study was better suited to the system than either of the oat varieties. Barley gave a similar DM production to oats but was better fermented, reflecting its higher content of WSC and DM. When cut at the dough stage the barley also allowed better aftermath growth of the undersown grass/clover. The results suggest this difference may be attributed to a more open canopy in the barley crop and that the barley variety used reached the milk and dough stages some 9 to 14 days earlier than the oats. It should be emphasised that this study was confined to only one variety of barley, naked oat and husked oat. Other varieties of both cereals may well have ensiling and growth characteristics better suited to the system.

Acknowledgements

We are grateful to the Analytical Chemistry Unit, IGER, Aberystwyth, for the chemical analyses and to Semundo Ltd. for the oat seed.

References

BENNETT R.M. (1998) A review of the potential for the production and utilization of oats in the United Kingdom. *A report to MAFF and the HGCA by the Centre for Agricultural Strategy.*

IGER (1996) Conversion to organic milk production. *IGER Technical Review No. 4.*

LAWES, D.A. and JONES D.I.H (1971) Yield, nutritive value and ensiling characteristics of whole-crop spring cereals. *Journal of Agricultural Science, Cambridge,* **76**, 479-485.

SIEFERS M.K., HUCK G.L., YOUNG M.A., TURNER J.E., PENDERGRAFT J.J., ANDERSON S.A. and BOLSEN K.K. (1996) Agronomic and silage quality traits of winter cereals. In: Jones D.I.H., Jones R., Dewhurst R., Merry R. and Haigh P.M. (eds.) *Proceedings of the 11th Silage Conference,* Aberystwyth, pp.152-153.

TETLOW R.M. (1990) A decade of research into whole-crop cereals at Hurley. In: Wilkinson J.M. and Stark B.A. (ed.) *Whole-Crop Cereals, Making and Feeding Cereal Silage,* pp. 1-17. Chalcombe Publications, UK.

Chapter 12

Economics of Forage Crops

D. Gardner

GENUS Consultancy, Westmere Drive, Crewe CW1 1ZD

Summary

Increased output of milk from forage is reflected in higher margin per litre of milk, but the relationship between milk output from forage and profit is more complex. The cost of producing forages for silage depends on crop yield. Higher milk yield per cow and higher milk protein contents cost money to produce. Grazed grass, the cheapest feed, is often substituted by buffer feeds of considerably higher cost. Changes to alternative forages may result in increased overhead costs which reduce profit.

Cost of production

The key attraction of forage crops is that they should be cheaper to grow than any bought in or manufactured substitute feed (Table 12.1).

Making more use of forage is a logical way of keeping more of the milk cheque to yourself, at a time of high milk quota prices and a fall in milk prices. This can also be shown by looking at those who do achieve high production from forage (Table 12.2).

At a forage enthusiasts' conference, I could probably stop here. The case is made: more milk from forage equals more profit! Whilst generally true, for the individual farmer, the situation is more complex.

Table 12.1   Production costs of different feeds

	Cost of dry matter (£/tonne)
Grazed grass/clover	10
Grazed grass	17
Maize silage	42
Perennial grass silage	47
Fodder beet	47
Whole-crop wheat silage	53
Brewers' grains	120
Dairy compound	200

Table 12.2   Effect of increasing milk production from forage on margin per litre of milk

	National average	Milkminder average	Top 20%	Top 1%
Milk from forage (l)	1820	2590	3875	5190
Yield per cow (l)	5350	6340	6505	6905
Feed use per cow (kg)	1700	1780	1267	830
Margin per litre (£)	20.0	21.2	22.2	23.2
Extra value per cow above average (£)	-	70	143	228

The costs shown in Table 12.1 assume contract costs for all field operations, and optimum crop yields, but does everyone get "optimum" yields? The effect of yield on costs of production is much greater for crops which are only cut for silage compared to those which are only grazed (Figure 12.1).

Figure 12.1   Costs of production in relation to crop yield

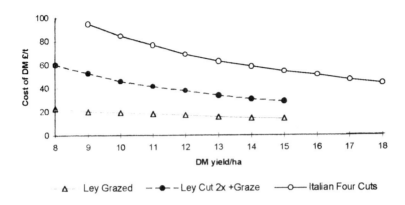

A low yielding maize crop (9 t DM/ha) is actually considerably dearer than a high yielding crop of Italian ryegrass cut 4 times for silage. From our farm survey work we have found that nearly half of those growing maize achieve yields only of 9 tonnes DM per hectare.

Furthermore, remember that these figures are all using full contract costs, for a fair comparison. However many of you are geared up for grass silage, with forager, trailers and tractors. When you decide to grow maize, you are certainly going to get the contractor to precision-drill and harvest your crop. But are you going to sell some of your machinery, or sack half a man because of the contractor coming in? Almost certainly no, so the decision to grow maize generates **extra** overhead costs.

Alternative forages

To justify a change from good grass silage to an alternative forage, there have to be clear advantages, in crop production, in risk, or in rewards, for the real cost differences between different crops when grown for silage are nearly negligible.

83

One such trial often cited is the excellent MMB-funded CEDAR research into alternative forages. For simplicity, I'll only refer to the grass and maize part of the three-year trial, in Table 12.3.

Table 12.3 **Effect of mixed forage diets on forage intake, milk production and intake value (from Browne *et al.*, 1995)**

	Grass only	**33% maize**	**75% maize**
Forage intake (kg/day)	10.2	12.4	12.8
Milk yield[1] (l/day)	20.9	24.0	27.4
Milk protein (%)	3.03	3.14	3.16
Milk butterfat (%)	4.15	4.04	3.90
Milk value (£/day)	4.18	4.96	5.06

[1] with 6 kg concentrate per cow per day

At face value the extra output is worth £100/cow, as both higher yields and better milk quality. But:

- Few herds have only fresh-calved cows to feed this expensive silage to!
- All farmers I know would have to buy quota.
- The extra milk yield and milk protein content cost money.
- Most herdsmen would "chase" the extra yield of the cows by feeding more compound.

The **real** economic benefit of maize and whole-crop, is that they allow the dry hot south and east regions to compete with those who can grow grass well in the wetter west and north! It's as daft trying to grow maize in Cumbria as it is to rely on ryegrass swards on the Dorset chalk downs or on the Hampshire sands! I remain a real fan of maize for that reason alone! The real economic advantage of whole-crop cereals is risk management: a cold dry year, and into the silo it goes, or given a wet warm grassy year and plenty of grass silage, then the combine gets it instead.

The real costs of milk production

What is the economic benefit of grazing?

- It is far cheaper (Table 12.1 and Figure 12.1).
- Grazing pollutes less, with no effluent and less carbon dioxide and nitrates.
- Grazing is the image that your milk and meat buyers want - and one day might pay for.

The real benefit of grazing grass depends on just what your own real costs of silage are - usually £60 to £70/t DM. Buffer feeding at grass often means that the cow substitutes easily-eaten forage in the ring feeder for walking and grazing. Buffer feeding should substitute for purchased concentrates.

We are in danger of forgetting the **whole** costs of milk production, for margin over concentrates bears too little relationship to profit.

If changing from an all-grass diet to a mixed silage diet, also means changing the trough feeds, making an "investment" in other costs such as a complete diet machine, loaders, block cutters and another silo store, then there are major increases to overhead costs, and these so easily reduce profit (Table 12.4). Grazed crops can make real inroads to the machinery, labour and financing costs that make up much of that 20ppl "other costs" (Table 12.4).

Table 12.4   The real costs of milk production (pence per litre, ppl)

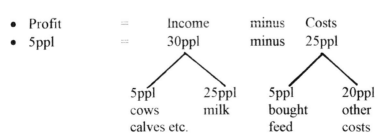

- Profit   =   Income   minus   Costs
- 5ppl   =   30ppl   minus   25ppl

5ppl cows calves etc.	25ppl milk	5ppl bought feed	20ppl other costs

Conclusion

Finally we should all remember that the dairy is but one part of a whole farm business. Not every farm has the resources, or the skills, to farm in the same way. For example, the superb high yield from forage story shown in Table 21.2, top 1%, is exactly right for the low stocking rate, grassy farm with too little quota. However each of his cows need to be offered 5.7 tonnes of forage dry matter to achieve this level of substitution for bought feed in comparison to the 4.2 tonnes of "the average". If you were able to grow 20 tonnes of sugar beet per acre, or 4 tonnes of milling wheat, you would probably be right to look at this rather differently!

That's what farm business management is all about.

Reference

BROWNE I., ALLEN D., PHIPPS R.H. and SUTTON J.D. (1995) *Mixed Forage Diets for Dairy Cows*. UK Milk Development Council.

Chapter 13

The Integration of White Clover and Other Forage Crops into Whole Farm Systems

J.A. Bax

SAC Crichton Royal Farm, Mid Park, Bankend Road,
Dumfries DG1 4SZ

Summary

The yield of DM from grass/white clover swards in the west of Scotland has ranged from 0.65 to 0.97 of that of grass swards which received up to 340 kg N/ha. The performance of clover-rich swards is influenced by the extent to which slurry is used, and soil temperature in the winter period. The tactical use of fertiliser N may be appropriate to boost the growth of grass/clover swards following a cold winter. Changing from grass to grass/white clover requires additional land to support the same livestock population. Undersowing a spring cereal crop is the preferred route for the introduction of clover into the farm system. Alternative forage crops can complement grass and grass/white clover swards. The choice of crop depends on the extent to which additional energy, protein or starch is required. The potential animal production benefit from alternative forages depends on the quality of the basal grass silage and the quality of the alternative forage. With high-quality grass silage the response to mixed forage diets may be small. Possibly the greatest potential for alternative forages is in low-input systems where it is vital to buffer animal variations in grass production and thus maintain an adequate supply of forage of high quality.

Introduction

Swards rich in white clover can form the basis of successful dairy systems in the UK. They have the potential to reduce forage production costs and can improve animal performance. In practice the extent of any benefits will be influenced by a combination of factors including the productivity of the swards, the manner in which they are utilised and the associated cost structure of the farm system. There are however alternative forage crops which have the potential for integration in clover-based systems, or those with conventional grass and nitrogen fertiliser. The forages can be used to secure forage supply where grass growth may be limited or to manipulate animal performance. In some cases the cost of alternative forages can be less than for grass silage, and they can therefore be used to reduce the total cost of forage production on the farm. Where it is physically possible to develop a multiple forage approach it may be more appropriate to grow the optimum combination of forages required to achieve the desired level of milk production and composition.

It is generally accepted that white clover based dairy systems can support stocking rates of up to 2.0 livestock units (LU)/ha, with herbage outputs of between 80 and 95% of those achieved with grass swards receiving up to 340 kg N/ha/annum. In practice, there are currently few dairy systems in the UK that are totally reliant on grass/clover swards which can be vulnerable to the consequences of poor growth in early season. Various management strategies can be employed to overcome this potential problem including the use of strategic inorganic nitrogen fertiliser applications, the retention of grass/N swards on part of the farm, or the use of alternative forage crops. This paper will describe the potential for developing the use of white clover and other forage crops in animal productions systems.

Forage production potential

The production potential of grass/white clover swards has been extensively reviewed (Bax and Browne, 1995; Davies and Hopkins, 1996; Frame and Newbold, 1984). Estimates range from 5 to 10 t DM/ha. The yield of herbage is influenced by a range of factors including fertiliser and slurry use, the time of cutting and the clover content of the sward.

Roberts *et al.* (1989) compared a grass/N sward receiving up to 340 kg N/annum with a grass/white clover sward under a three-cut silage regime over a four-year period. No mineral or organic nitrogen fertiliser was applied to the clover-rich sward, but both sward types received between 69 and 120 kg P_2O_5 and between 100 and 290 K_2O annually. The DM yield of the clover-rich sward ranged from 0.65 to 0.78 of that achieved by the grass/N sward.

In a subsequent long-term dairy system study at SAC's Crichton Royal Farm, grass/white clover swards (zero inorganic N) have achieved between 0.74 and 0.97 of the dry matter yield over three cuts compared to grass/N swards receiving up to 340 kg N/ha/annum. In both cases the lower relative yield achieved in certain years was attributed to cold weather in the spring which depressed clover growth and vigour. The higher relative yields of grass/clover silage in the system study compared to the results of Roberts *et al.* (1989) were attributed to the use of slurry on the swards.

All of the grazing and conservation requirements for one herd in the Acrehead system study, currently supporting 70 cows and their youngstock have been provided by grass/white clover swards since 1988. During this period no purchased nitrogen fertiliser has been used at all. However, there has been a wide variation in early season herbage production as indicated by first cut silage yields which have ranged from 2.4 t DM/ha to 5.9 t DM/ha. An analysis of the weather data during this period has shown a clear relationship between soil temperature (at 30 cm depth) in January/February/March and the subsequent yield of first cut silage (see Figure 13.1).

The use of inorganic nitrogen fertiliser will increase the production of herbage from clover-rich swards, but it also has a deleterious effect on clover content (Frame, 1996). The use of tactical inputs of inorganic nitrogen has been advocated as a means of increasing herbage production whilst minimising the risk of reducing the clover content of the sward (Frame and Boyd 1987). Reported herbage responses to strategic inorganic nitrogen inputs have been variable and are probably influenced by weather conditions (Laidlaw and Stewart, 1987). Frame (1996) reported that in each year over a five-year period nitrogen applications increased grass dry matter yield from a grass/clover sward compared to a zero N clover-rich sward. Although clover contents were reduced, the use of inorganic N did not have a significant long-term effect. However, if soil temperature could be used as a guide, it would be possible to restrict the use of strategic N fertiliser applications to those seasons when a zero N strategy was likely to result in a reduced dry matter yield at first cut. For the 1997 harvest year in the Acrehead system study, it is proposed that a tactical application of N fertiliser will be applied if the mean January-March soil temperature at 30 cm is below 5 C, to ensure an adequate DM yield at first cut.

Figure 13.1   Relationship between mean soil temperature between January and March and first cut silage yield

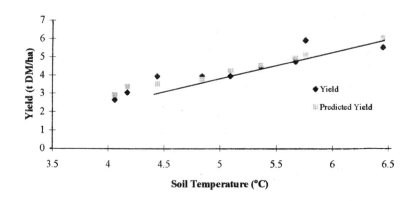

In recent years there has been considerable interest in the use of alternative forages as a means to complement grass silage or in the more extreme cases to replace it altogether. The most common alternatives are forage maize and whole-crop cereals whilst other crops such as **kale**

are becoming more popular again as new harvesting techniques are developed. The decision as to whether a crop should be grown will initially be determined by the suitability of the soil type and climate. Other factors that need to be taken into account include the potential yield, the risk associated with growing the crop, the cost per unit of energy or protein, whether it is an appropriate feed and whether it can be integrated into the whole farm system. Labour implications and machinery/contractor requirements will also need to be considered.

The potential yield of a range of forage crops is illustrated in Table 13.1.

Table 13.1   Potential yield of the major forage crops

	DM (t/ha)	ME (GJ/ha)	CP (kg/ha)
PRG	10	110	1580
PRG/white clover	9	97	1260
IRG/red clover	10	113	1575
Lucerne	12	115	2300
Forage maize	12	132	1080
Whole-crop wheat	13	126	1080
Whole-crop barley	11	107	945
Fodder beet (roots)	14	162	810
Stubble turnips	4	52	540
Kale	8	88	1216
Forage peas	8	89	1490

PRG = perennial ryegrass, IRG = Italian ryegrass

The area of forage maize has increased rapidly with an estimated 100,000 ha grown in 1996. The crop is relatively simple to grow, does not need to be in a crop rotation and can yield in excess of 4 t of starch DM/ha. With the advent of better ensiling techniques and additives, similar yields of starch can be achieved with both the fermented and alkaline preserved forms of whole-crop cereals in areas where maize is not a viable crop. Possibly the most underrated crop in the UK is fodder beet which can outyield all other crops on an energy basis. However potential difficulties with weed control and harvesting have limited its popularity. Increased feed protein costs have revived interest in crops such as forage peas, red clover and lucerne which have been in decline for a number of years. With the advent of new ensiling techniques such as big bale kale (kaleage) and whole-cropping of forage peas, there are new possibilities to exploit these crops. The choice of crop will be influenced by whether, for example, additional energy, protein or starch is required.

Introducing white clover into a farm system

The techniques exist successfully to convert a conventionally-managed all grass/N system entirely to clover-rich swards receiving zero nitrogen fertiliser inputs within a 12-month period without incurring a reduction in animal performance (Bax and Tiley, 1989). However, most producers would be advised to approach a conversion in stages to reduce the element of risk at crop establishment and to adapt to the management requirements of a grass/clover system. It is recognised that changing to a clover-based system requires additional land if a similar output of animal production is to be maintained without the use of extra purchased feeds. In the case of the Acrehead system study an additional 25% more land was allocated to make up the shortfall in forage production. (Bax and Thomas, 1991). There is a range of methods available to establish white clover, including direct reseeding, direct drilling or oversowing into an established grass ward and undersowing in cereals. It is also possible to encourage the proliferation of existing but low clover contents in grass swards (Bax and Browne, 1995). Generally the simpler techniques can be less reliable and the clover may take longer to establish. If a vigorous clover establishment is not achieved the productivity of the sward will be reduced initially, particularly if minimal or zero inputs of purchased nitrogen are intended. Undersowing a spring cereal crop is a popular method of establishing a grass/clover ley, particularly when the crop is cut early for ensiling as whole-crop. This both reduces the risk of lodging, which can seriously damage the developing ley, and can also compensate for the lost forage production incurred with a direct spring reseed. Although direct reseeding can be carried out from April to mid August, later reseeding should be timed to ensure good clover establishment before growth slows in the autumn. It is important to specify the type of clovers to match the system and to use the newer improved varieties. Recent UK bred varieties AberHerald and AberCrest in particular have improved winter hardiness and the ability to commence or maintain active growth at lower temperatures. The use of combinations of clover types in a sward permits greater flexibility in its subsequent management and utilisation.

Utilising alternative forage crops

The incorporation of forage crops into grass-based systems can be as simple as an undersown grass re-seed in spring barley for conservation as whole-crop silage or an area of continual maize cropping. The inclusion of other crops such as fodder beet creates more complications as a rotation may be required to avoid disease problems. If the whole farm system already has an arable component it is relatively straightforward to develop alternative forage crops. However, as with all new enterprises there will be a learning curve and advice should be sought to minimise the risk of any potential problems, particularly if there is little experience of growing crops other than grass.

The potential animal production benefit from incorporating alternative forages in the diet will be influenced both by the quality of the basal grass silage and by the quality of the alternative forage. In a recent experiment at SAC's Crichton Royal Farm the response of high-yielding dairy cows fed high quality grass silage (GS) to alternative forages was determined. Either maize silage (MS), fermented whole-crop wheat (FWC) or urea treated whole-crop wheat (UWC) was incorporated with grass silage at 40% of the forage dry matter intake. The composition of the feeds is shown in Table 13.2.

Table 13.2   Composition of forages

	GS	MS	FWC	UWC
DM (g/kg)	248	275	557	791
CP (g/kg DM)	132	94	89	183
ME (MJ/kg DM)	11.4	10.9	10.7	11.4
Ammonia (g/kg DM)	28	37	33	73
pH	3.6	3.7	4.0	8.4
Starch (g/kg DM)	29	256	359	373
Water soluble carbohydrate (g/kg DM)	46	8.2	3.1	1.4

The grass silage was well-fermented and had an intake factor of 116%. The maize silage was close to the optimum dry matter and contained 256 g of starch/kg DM. Both types of whole-crop wheat had starch contents in excess of 350 g/kg DM. All the alternative forages significantly increased total forage dry matter and total dry matter intake (Table 13.3).

Table 13.3   Feed intake and animal performance

	GS	GS+MS	GS+FWC	GS+UWC	Sig
Forage dry matter intake (kg/d)	10.6	11.4	12.2	13.1	**
Total dry matter intake (kg/d)	17.6	18.4	19.2	20.1	**
Milk yield (kg/d)	27.4	26.4	27.1	26.9	NS
Milk fat (g/kg)	48.9	46.9	49.0	48.1	NS
Milk protein (g/kg)	34.1	33.6	34.0	34.3	NS

Mean milk yields over the four-month experimental period were high on all treatments, with no advantage gained from the incorporation of either maize or whole-crop cereals. Similarly, the high milk protein level achieved on the grass silage was not improved further by the addition of alternative forages. However in other experiments where the basal grass silage was of a moderate quality, milk yield and milk protein responses to the inclusion of single alternative forages were observed (Phipps, 1996).

Alternative forages were included in the management of the Acrehead system study for 1996/97. Previously the only home-grown forage was grass or grass/white clover. The system study is investigating the relative performance of a low input/moderate output (LI) dairy system with a moderate input/high output (HO) system. The design is shown in Table 13.4.

Table 13.4   Design of the 1996/97 Acrehead system study

	Low input	High output
Land area (ha)	46	46
Herd size	70	70
Stocking rate (LU/ha)	2.0	2.0
Sward type	grass/white clover	grass
Fertiliser N (kg/ha)	0	<250
Target milk sales (l/cow)	5500	9000
Target concentrate use (kg/l)	<0.09	<0.24
Milking frequency	2x	3x
Alternative forages	yes	yes

LU = livestock unit

Both herds, which calve 50:50 autumn and spring, are managed by the same herdsman and each herd rears its own youngstock. Whole-crop barley and fodder beet were grown for the low input herd using no purchased fertiliser and minimal chemical inputs. Whole-crop wheat and fodder beet were grown for the high output herd. The alternative forages were introduced into the low input system to increase the total yield of conserved forage and to provide a potential means to manipulate milk composition in a very low concentrate input management system.

Their role in the high output system is to assist in increasing total dry matter intake as higher milk yields are sought without penalising milk composition. The DM yields of whole-crop barley and wheat were 10.6 and 10.9 t/ha. Both were spring sown crops. The DM yields of fodder beet were 10.5 and 9.4 t DM/ha respectively for the low input and high output system. The introduction of alternative forages resulted in an additional 40 t DM of conserved feed for the low input herd over the previous year without the use of any purchased fertiliser.

Preliminary results suggest that a multiple forage diet, can be used to maintain a high level of milk protein during the winter feeding period when low levels of concentrate are offered, 1 to 2 kg/ha/day from calving for autumn calved cows and 0.5 kg/ha/day for spring calved cows (Figure 13.2).

Figure 13.2   Milk protein content: Acrehead low input herd, 1994/95 to 1996/97

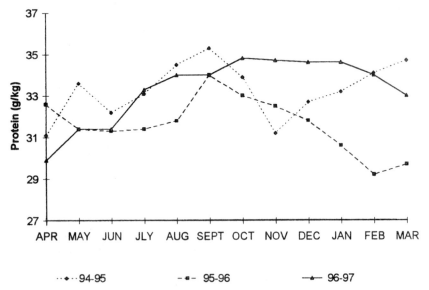

The mean October 1996 to January 1997 milk protein content was 34.7 g/kg. The previous winter, milk protein declined steadily from housing to a low point of 29.5 g/kg in February as a consequence of insufficient grass/clover silage. In 1994/95 by contrast the availability of excellent quality grass/clover silage (DM 444 g/kg, ME 12.5 MJ/kg DM, FME/ME 0.84 enabled milk protein levels to be raised from a post calving low of 31.2 g/kg to 34.7 g/kg in the following March. In a low input system where forage quality and quantity is of such importance, alternative forages could play an important role in buffering the year-to-year variations in grass silage that occur.

Conclusions

There is considerable scope to increase the use of white clover and other forage crops in whole farm systems in the UK. They can be used to reduce the level of external inputs required in a dairy system and have considerable scope to improve animal performance. New growing and conservation techniques have increased their potential uptake. Further developments such as bi-cropping and growing combinations of crops for ensiling may extend the possibilities further. In situations where grass growth may be limited, alternative forage crops can be used effectively to maintain animal performance. Multiple forage feeding strategies offer a means to increase feed intake where high milk yields are being sought, and can be used to improve milk composition in production systems with low concentrate inputs. The extent of their uptake will also be influenced however by the milk price:concentrate ratio, which currently favours the continued use of purchased concentrates.

References

BAX J A. and BROWNE I. (1995) *The Use of Clover on Dairy Farms.* Milk Development Council, London.

BAX J.A. and THOMAS C. (1991) Developments in legume use for milk production. In: Hopkins A (ed.) *Grass on the Move.* Occasional Symposium of the British Grassland Society, No 26, pp. 40-53.

BAX J.A. and TILEY G.E.D. (1989) The establishment of a white clover based dairy system. In: *Environmentally Responsible*

Grassland Management, Winter Meeting of the British Grassland Society, Poster 20.

DAVIES D.A. and HOPKINS A. (1996) Production benefits of legumes in grassland. In: Younie D. (ed.) *Legumes in Sustainable Farming Systems*. Occasional Symposium of the British Grassland Society, No 30, pp. 234-246.

FRAME J. and NEWBOULD P. (1984) Herbage production from grass/white clover swards. In: Thomson D J (ed.) *Forage Legumes*. Occasional Symposium of the British Grassland Society, No 16, pp. 15-35.

FRAME J. (1996) The effect of fertiliser nitrogen application in spring and/or autumn on the production from a perennial ryegrass/white clover sward. In: *Recent Research and Development on White Clover in Europe*. REUR Technical series 42, ROME:FAO, pp. 88-91.

FRAME J. and BOYD A.G. (1987) The effect of strategic use of fertiliser nitrogen in spring and/or autumn on the productivity of a perennial ryegrass/white clover sward. *Grass and Forage Science* 42, pp. 429-438.

LAIDLAW A.S. and STEWART T.A. (1987) Clover development in the sixth to ninth year of grass/clover sward as affected by out of season management and spring nitrogen fertiliser application. *Research and Development in Agriculture*, 4, pp. 155-160.

ROBERTS D.J., FRAME J. and LEAVER J.D. (1989). A comparison of a grass/white clover sward with a grass sward plus fertiliser nitrogen under a three cut silage regime. *Research and Development in Agriculture* 6, pp. 147-150.

Chapter 14

Poster Papers

Growing and Conserving Kale/Barley as a Bi-Crop

N.E. Young

*Institute of Grassland and Environmental Research,
North Wyke, Okehampton, Devon, EX20 2SB*

Summary

Kale and barley drilled simultaneously in strips of variable width were ensiled either 14 or 16 weeks after sowing. Yield of DM 14 weeks after sowing was highest when the area of land occupied by barley was 75%. Dry matter content of barley increased substantially between the first and second harvest. All silages were well-preserved with contents of estimated ME in the range of 11.5 to 12.7 MJ/kg DM. Bi-crops of kale and barley show promise, especially for areas where maize is not a viable alternative.

Introduction

The low dry matter (DM) content of kale (ca. 150 g/kg) means that without substantial wilting, which leads to high field losses, it is difficult to ensile. Some 82% of all silage in England and Wales is made in bunker and clamp silos, thus raising the DM concentration of the kale silage by combining it with another high DM crop would appear to be an appropriate technique to study.

Small plot studies

In 1995, kale (Pinfold) and barley (Cooper) were drilled simultaneously but in strips occupying different areas of land (sowing rates 8.6 and 137 kg/ha respectively). This was achieved by using a combination drill and shutting off the appropriate spouts to obtain the different sowing proportions. Crops were drilled on 21st April and harvested when the barley was at the soft cheese stage (14 weeks post sowing - 27 July) and at the hard grain stage (16 weeks post sowing - 9 August). The crops were cut and wilted for 24 hours prior to harvesting with a forage harvester and the material packed into 40 litre barrels as mini silos. It can be seen from Table 14.1 that the highest yields were when the barley was a high proportion of the total crop. At the harvest taken 16 weeks after sowing, yields had increased substantially in the 50% and 75% kale crops due to its increasing as a proportion of the total. The barley by this stage would have stopped increasing in yield but the DM% of both crops had risen, particularly the barley.

Table 14.1   Yield of kale/barley bi-crop

	Proportion of area sown to kale	DM content of kale (g/kg)	DM content of barley (g/kg)	DM yield of total crop (t/ha)
Harvested 14	25%	200	451	9.7
weeks	50%	200	458	6.7
after sowing	75%	197	462	5.8
Harvested 16	25%	239	756	9.6
weeks	50%	239	717	8.9
after sowing	75%	235	701	7.6

The nutritional values of the crops are shown in Table 14.2. At the 14 weeks harvest the DM% of the silages were quite high, the lower values occurring where the kale proportion was highest. The pH and ammonia nitrogen (NH_3N) values both reflect a satisfactory fermentation especially as no additive was used. Crude protein levels at 130 g/kg were high but did not show the anticipated increase due to the higher proportion of kale in the crop. The ME values should be treated with caution as no entirely satisfactory method exists at present for analysing this material. The values for the 16-week harvest showed a rapid and substantial increase in DM as the barley ripened and the NH_3N values were particularly low in these cuts. The crude protein and ME levels declined somewhat from the harvest made 2 weeks earlier.

Table 14.2 Analysis of kale/barley bi-crop silage

	Proportion of area sown to kale	DM g/kg	pH	NH₃N g/kg	WSC* g/kg	Crude protein g/kg DM	ME MJ/kg DM
Harvested	25%	342	4.0	59	13.0	137	12.5
14 weeks	50%	264	4.0	64	12.7	142	12.4
after sowing	75%	234	4.0	67	12.7	134	11.5
Harvested	25%	588	5.0	19	20.4	126	12.7
16 weeks	50%	460	4.9	21	31.5	128	12.3
after sowing	75%	301	4.5	35	51.8	131	12.2

*Water soluble carbohydrate

Larger-scale trial

In 1996 we opted for the 50:50 mix of kale/barley and grew 5.5 ha. The driest June and July for the past 30 years depressed the yield of kale but following rainfall in late August the kale crop grew rapidly. An evaluation of this crop compared with grass silage is being undertaken at North Wyke using spring calving dairy cows.

Conclusions

These crops have produced substantial amounts of DM in relatively short periods of time. We still have much to learn about the most appropriate combination of crops and growing methods but we believe that the high yields of metabolizable energy and crude protein make this crop worthy of serious consideration especially in areas where maize is not a viable alternative.

The Effects of Offering Big-Bale Kale Silage to Dairy Cows

N.E. Young

*Institute of Grassland and Environmental Research,
North Wyke, Okehampton, Devon, EX20 2SB*

Summary

Kale ensiled in big bales was given to spring-calving dairy cows as the basal forage feed together with grass silage (50:50), in comparison with grass silage alone. The kale silage had a lower DM content than the grass silage and grass silage was apparently more palatable than the kale silage. Yields of milk and of milk constituents were similar for grass silage and the kale/grass silage mixture. Cows rejected thicker kale stems.

Introduction

Kale is a versatile crop which can be sown from April through to early July and is particularly valuable on dairy farms as:-

- it enables utilization of large amounts of slurry;
- it can be grazed or conserved;
- conserving the crop enables rapid clearance of the field and establishment of the following crop;
- it can be harvested with conventional grassland machinery;
- it produces 5 to 6 tonnes of dry matter in 12 to 14 weeks;
- it has a protein content of c. 17% and a sugar content which rises to c.25% as the crop matures.

The technical process of conserving the kale in big bales is now well proven but little work has been undertaken to evaluate the crop as a feed for dairy cows.

Assessments

In this work 10 multiparous spring-calving Holstein-Friesian dairy cows, initially between weeks 6 and 13 of lactation, were offered, individually, a 50:50 mix of kale and grass silage. Their performance and intake was compared with 10 similar cows offered grass silage alone for a period of 7 weeks. Both groups received 3 kg of a 22% protein concentrate twice daily during milking.

The silages were weighed and mixed by hand and, due to the bulk of the kale silage, were offered to the cows three times daily. Refusals were removed daily, weighed and sampled and the grass:kale samples were separated into the two fractions.

Milk yields were recorded at each milking and samples for milk composition taken weekly. The cows were weighed and condition scored weekly.

Results

The kale silage was considerably lower in DM than the grass silage, but had a higher ME and protein content (Table 14.3).

Table 14.3 Analysis of grass/kale silage

	Grass silage	Kale silage
DM (g/kg)	296	154
pH	4.1	4.5
DOMD (g/kg DM)	671	692
ME (MJ/kg DM)	10.8	11.1
Crude protein (g/kg DM)	150	196
Ash (g/kg DM)	90	180
Soluble nitrogen (g/kg DM)	157	268

The intake of the grass:kale mix was lower (by 1.44 kg/day) than the grass silage alone (see Table 14.4), but the difference was not significant. It is also interesting to note that the intake of grass silage was higher than for kale silage where both were on offer.

Table 14.4 Intake, milk yield and milk composition

	Grass silage	Grass and kale silage
DM Intake (kg/day)		
Grass silage	12.7	7.0
Kale silage	-	4.31
Total forage	12.7	11.3
Milk yield (kg/day)	30.40	29.35
Milk fat (g/kg)	40.1	39.1
Milk protein (g/kg)	28.4	28.8
Milk lactose (g/kg)	48.0	48.0
Yield of milk fat (kg/day)	1.213	1.145
Yield of milk protein (kg/day)	0.854	0.846
Yield of milk lactose (kg/day)	1.46	1.41

There were no significant differences in milk yield or milk composition despite the lower DM intake. Also the cows on the kale silage apparently gained more weight than the cows on the grass silage alone (18 kg vs. 7 kg) though the differences were not significant. There was no evidence of kale anaemia or of taint in the milk which is sometimes associated with feeding kale.

Conclusions

The kale silage was of high nutritive value compared with the grass silage in respect of ME and crude protein and was readily consumed, but there appeared to be a preference for grass silage when both were on offer. Despite the lower DM intakes on grass/kale, milk yields were only slightly depressed and there were no differences between groups in liveweight change or condition score. The tendency for fat concentrations to be depressed and that for protein to increase is of interest and could be a valuable management tool for dairy farmers. The preference of the cows for the leaf fraction of the kale plant and rejection of thicker stems endorses the requirement for a high plant population when growing the crop to maximise leaf to stem ratio.

Effect of Date of Harvest on the Composition of Kale Ensiled as Round Bales

R. Fychan and R. Jones

Institute of Grassland and Environmental Research,
Plas Gogerddan, Aberystwyth, Ceredigion, SY23 3EB

Summary

Kale was cut and ensiled as round bales after 15, 18 and 20 weeks of growth. The dry matter and water soluble carbohydrates content of the crop increased as the crop matured, whilst the crude protein and buffering capacity decreased. Delaying the harvest until 18 and 20 weeks of growth significantly improved silage fermentation (reduced pH and ammonia-N levels) when compared to the 15-week silage but did not affect digestibility or energy content. Dry matter losses during ensiling were also reduced for the later-cut crops.

Introduction

Early reports on kale silage (Kirsch and Jantzon, 1935) showed advantages in nutritional quality of kale silage in terms of crude protein and digestibility compared to grass silage. More recent reports have shown that preserving kale at 16 weeks of growth as round bale silage produced excellent fermentation characteristics with low pH and ammonia-N levels (Jones *et al.*, 1996). The present study investigated the effect of stages of maturity of kale at harvest on fermentation characteristics, silage quality and in-silo dry matter loss.

Materials and methods

A kale mixture ('Kaleage', Sharpes International, cv. Pinfold and Keeper) was drilled into a firm, fine seedbed on the 2 May 1996 at 7.5 kg/ha. FYM was applied (40 tonnes/ha) before ploughing and 62 kg N, 12kg P_2O_5 and 12 kg K_2O/ha of an inorganic fertiliser was applied to the seedbed. At 6-weeks growth 1 kg/ha Desmetryn was applied for the control of broad-leaved weeds and N fertiliser (42 kg N/ha) was also applied. The kale was mown 100 mm above ground level after 15, 18 and 20 weeks of growth using a disc mower and the cut kale was left to wilt undisturbed for two days. Five bales were ensiled on each maturity date using a Greenland RF120 fixed chamber baler. All bales were sampled for chemical composition and weighed for yield estimation immediately after baling. Bales were wrapped in six layers of film wrap before being stored unstacked under cover. After 90 days ensiling all the bales were again sampled for silage analysis and weighed to estimate dry matter loss.

Results

The kale crop was well established with a mean plant population at cutting of 97.8 plants/m^2. Kale chemical composition and yield at harvest (15, 18 and 20 weeks of growth) are shown in Table 14.5. Dry matter (DM) content tended to increase as the kale crop matured from 15 to 20 weeks. During this period crude protein content and buffering capacity decreased significantly and there was a marked and highly significant increase in water soluble carbohydrates (WSC) content. This increase of 77% in WSC from 15 to 20 weeks (an increase from 16 g/kg to 31 g/kg on a fresh weight basis), accompanied by a significant drop in buffering capacity, indicates a much better ensiling potential for the more mature cuts. DOMD values predicted from pepsin-cellulase solubility using a grass equation indicated little change in digestibility between 15 and 20 weeks of growth.

Baled silage composition and in-bale DM losses are shown in Table 14.6. Silage made at the 18 and 20-week harvest were well preserved. Silage pH, ammonia-N and acetic acid levels were significantly lower and lactic acid higher than in the silages made at 15 weeks. S-methyl cysteine sulphoxide (SMCO) content was relatively low at 5.5 g/kg DM with no significant difference between the harvest dates. The results in Table 14.6 indicate that DM losses decreased markedly by delaying harvest date but the differences were not statistically significant. This was due to a large variation in DM content of individual bales within treatments.

Table 14.5   Yield of kale DM and composition (g/kg DM unless otherwise stated)

| | Harvest stage | | | | |
	15 weeks	18 weeks	20 weeks	s.e.d.	Sig.
Dry matter (g/kg)	156.2	163.1	167.5	5.24	NS
Crude protein	158.1^a	125.4^b	113.6^b	5.95	***
WSC	104.6^a	155.6^b	185.4^c	9.84	***
DOMD %	72.7	72.4	71.9	1.60	NS
Ash	143.2	137.8	134.8	5.67	NS
Buffering capacity (meq/kg DM)	775.5^a	725.6^{ab}	696.7^b	25.93	*
Baled DM yield (kg/ha)	6344	6677	6949		

Within rows, values with different superscripts differ significantly (P<0.05).
NS = not significant, * = P<0.05, *** = P<0.001.

Table 14.6   Kale silage composition and in-bale DM loss (g/kg DM unless otherwise stated

| | Harvest stage | | | | |
	15 Week	18 Week	20 Week	s.e.d.	Sig.
Dry matter (g/kg)	141.5^a	153.8^{ab}	164.2^b	6.71	*
pH	4.90^a	4.44^b	4.33^b	0.110	***
Ammonia (g/kg N)	118.8^a	66.5^b	56.8^b	9.46	***
Crude protein	210.6^a	163.4^b	147.3^c	6.41	***
WSC	20.7^a	34.3^b	42.6^b	5.37	**
ME (MJ/kg DM)	10.82	11.10	11.11	0.224	NS
Lactic acid	56.7	68.09	79.0	14.32	NS
Acetic acid	47.5^a	27.0^b	20.8^b	4.57	***
SMCO	5.66	5.46	5.44	0.80	NS
Dry matter loss (g/kg)	137.8	102.2	58.3	37.31	NS

Within rows, values with different superscripts differ significantly (p<0.05).
NS = not significant, * = P<0.05, ** = P<0.01, *** = P<0.001.

Conclusions

The results show that kale can be successfully ensiled as round bale silage but emphasise the need for harvest date to be delayed until WSC levels are sufficiently high for a successful fermentation. Delay in harvest did not adversely affect digestibility or energy content but protein levels were reduced. There was a trend towards lower DM losses during ensiling with delayed harvest.

References

KIRSCH W. And JANTZON H. (1935) Conservation of alternative crops. *Züchtungskunde,* **10**, 218.224.

JONES R., FYCHAN R. And YOUNG N.E. (1996) Conservation of kale as big bale silage. In: Jones D.I.H., Jones R., Dewhurst R., Merry R. and Haigh P.M. (eds.) *Proceedings of the 11th Silage Conference, Aberystwyth,* Sept 1996, pp.180-181.

Forage Maize Grown under Plastic

M.H. Davies[1], D. W. Deakin[1] and J. Hardy[2]

[1]ADAS Rosemaund, Preston Wynne, Hereford HR1 3PG
[2]Grainseed (Maize) Limited, Unit 3, Langton Green, Eye, Suffolk IP23 7HN

Summary

The potential of growing maize under plastic was evaluated at ADAS Rosemaund in 1993. Forage maize was drilled under plastic on 24 April (P1) and compared with conventionally-sown maize drilled on the same day (C1) and on 7 May (C2). The effect of the plastic was to increase crop dry matter yield by 2.3 and 1.9 t/ha compared with C1 and C2 respectively, and to advance harvest date by 21 days. Cob index and starch content were also increased with the plastic treatment. In 1994, three varieties of maize (cv. LG2080, Nancis, Dartis) were drilled under plastic on 22 April and conventionally on 5 May. Growing maize under plastic significantly decreased days to emergence (16.3 vs. 21.3 days), increased dry matter yield (11.9 vs. 10.8 t/ha) and increased dry matter content at harvest (37.0 vs. 28.1%), as well as cob index (58.1 vs. 52.3) and starch content (27.6 vs. 21.0%). It is concluded that although yield responses from growing maize under plastic do not balance the additional costs incurred, other benefits, such as earlier harvest and improved composition, may be important in farm situations.

Introduction

With the development of earlier maturing varieties of forage maize, and the recognised consistently high feed value of maize silage, there has been a recent large expansion in the UK acreage and an increased interest in husbandry practices that improve its reliability. Over a two-year period, the potential of growing maize under plastic was evaluated at ADAS Rosemaund.

Materials and methods

In 1993, forage maize (cv. LG2080, Botanis, Erlevo, Zentis) was drilled under plastic on 24 April (P1) and compared with maize drilled conventionally on the same day (C1) or 13 days later on 7 May (C2). The maize grown under plastic was harvested on 14 October, whereas both conventional treatments were harvested on 5 November. In 1994, three varieties of maize (cv. LG2080, Nancis, Dartis) were drilled under plastic (P1) on 22 April and conventionally on 5 May (C2). All plots were harvested on 27 September. In both years, cultivation before drilling, fertiliser and herbicide regimes were the same for all treatments.

Results

Drilling maize under plastic significantly reduced the period between sowing and 100% crop emergence from 27 and 25 days for C1 and C2 respectively to 17 days for P1 in the first year, and from 21 days (C2) to

16 days (P1) in the second year. Septometer measurements taken on 2 July 1993 showed more advanced plant growth associated with drilling the crop under plastic, with 83% of light being intercepted compared with only 45% and 40% on C1 and C2 respectively. Dry matter samples taken during the period 4 to 5 weeks pre-harvest in both years also demonstrated clearly the earlier maturity of the plots drilled under plastic, in terms of both a higher whole plant dry matter content and a higher cob index at all sampling dates.

Table 14.7   Yield and dry matter content of forage maize harvested

	Dry matter yield (t/ha)		Dry matter content (%)	
	1993	1994	1993	1994
Plastic (P1)	13.0	11.9	30.2	37.0
Conventional (C1)	10.7	-	32.5	-
Conventional (C2)	11.1	10.8	27.6	28.1
s.e.d.	0.49	0.95	0.55	1.00

The effect of the plastic in 1993 was to increase crop dry matter yield by 2.3 and 1.9 t/ha compared with C1 and C2 respectively (Table 14.7). In 1994, although the yield response to plastic was only 1.1 t/ha dry matter, the dry matter content of the P1 crop was 9% higher than C2 when harvested on the same date.

An additional effect of the plastic was to increase cob index at harvest from 44.5% (mean of C1 and C2) to 53.0% for P1, and to increase starch content of silage at feeding from 11.5% to 20.6% in 1993. The equivalent assessments in 1994 showed that cob index was increased from 52.3% to 58.1% and starch content from 21.0% to 30.1% for P1 compared with C2 respectively.

Conclusions

- Growing under plastic decreased the period between drilling and 100% crop emergence by 7 days on average, and advanced crop maturity to allow earlier harvesting.

- Crop yields were significantly increased from growing maize under plastic by 2.1 and 1.1 tonnes dry matter per hectare during the two years of this experiment.

- The plastic treatment increased cob index at harvest and starch content at feeding.

Although the yield response from growing maize under plastic (mean +1.6 t/ha) did not balance the additional costs incurred (£224/ha), other benefits may be important in farm situations. These include; the ability to produce a viable crop of maize in marginal areas, a higher value feed for ruminants, and earlier sowing of succeeding crops.

Effect of a Combined Inoculant Enzyme Additive on the DM Loss During Ensiling, Fermentation Characteristics, Nutritive Value and Aerobic Stability of Maize Silage

S. Harrison, R.H. Phipps and E. Owen

Centre for Dairy Research, The University of Reading, Arborfield Hall Farm, Arborfield, Reading RG2 9HX

Summary

Two experiments are reported in which maize of 250 (Expt 1) and 350 g/DM kg (Expt 2) was ensiled in minisilos (2.5 kg capacity) either untreated (T1) or treated (T2) with a combined inoculant/enzyme additive which contained **Lactobacillus plantarum, Pedioccus acidilactici, Lactoccus lactis lactis,** *clostridial bacteriophages, hemicellulase and cellulase enzymes. Additive treatment reduced DM losses during ensiling (P<0.01). Treated silage had higher lactic acid (Expt 2 P<0.05), acetic acid (Expt 2 P<0.05) and ethanol (Expt 1 P<0.05, Expt 2 P<0.01) concentrations, lower NDF contents (Expt 1*

P<0.05) and higher predicted M.E values (Expt 2 P<0.05) when compared to the untreated material. The additive improved aerobic stability.

Introduction

Due to the development of early maturing maize hybrids the area of maize grown for silage in the UK has increased markedly. Many farmers do not capitalise on the positive relationship between maize silage DM content and silage intake, as high DM crops are difficult to consolidate and therefore more susceptible to aerobic instability. As a result there is a tendency to opt for an earlier harvest to reduce the risk of aerobic instability both during the winter feeding period and when used as a buffer feed during the summer. The aim of the current study was to determine the effect of a combined inoculant/enzyme additive containing *Lactobacillus plantarum, Pediococcus acidilactici, Lactoccus lactis lactis,* clostridial bacteriophages, hemicellulase and cellulase enzymes, on the DM loss during ensiling, fermentation characteristics, nutritive value and aerobic stability of maize silage.

Materials and methods

Maize was harvested at 250 g/DM kg (Expt 1) and 350 g/DM kg (Expt 2), and ensiled in minisilos (2.5 kg capacity) either untreated (T1) or treated with 2 1 additive/t fresh material (T2), each with six replicates. The additive was applied using a hand-held sprayer and the silos were filled, weighed, sealed and left for approximately 100 days to complete the fermentation process. On opening the silos were reweighed to determine DM loss during ensiling. The fermentation characteristics and nutritive value of the silages were determined. Temperature change during a ten-day period was used to indicate the stability of the silage.

Results

Mean values for the DM loss during ensiling, fermentation characteristics and nutritive value, together with the appropriate *s.e.d* values are shown in Tables 14.8 and 14.9.

112

Figure 14.1   Temperature changes recorded over a ten-day period of exposure of treated and untreated silages to air

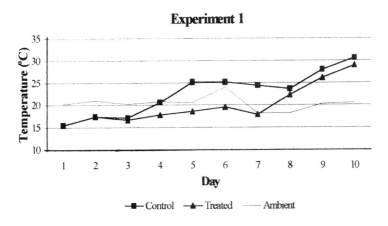

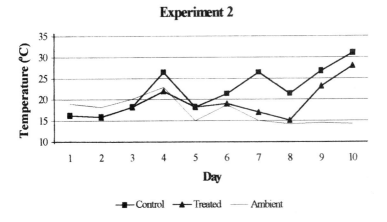

Treatment with the additive reduced DM losses during ensiling in both experiments (Expt 1 P<0.01). The treated silages had higher lactic and acetic acid concentrations (Expt 2 P<0.05), higher ethanol contents (Expt P<0.05, Expt 2 P<0.01), lower NDF contents (Expt 1 P<0.05) and higher predicted ME values (Expt 2 P<0.05) when compared to the untreated material. The temperature of the treated silage was significantly lower than the untreated silage on five of the ten days of measurement (Figure 14.1).

Table 14.8 Effec of an inoculant/enzyme additive on the fermentation characteristics of ensiled forage maize

Experiment	Treatment	DM loss	NH₃-N (g/kg TN)	pH	Composition (g/kg DM)				
					Lactic acid	Acetic acid	Propionic acid	Butyric acid	Ethanol
1	T1	128	76	3.8	84	10	<1	<1	16
	T2	46	68	3.8	85	15	<1	<1	19
	SED	38.6	4.5	0.03	3.6	0.9	-	-	1.2
2	T1	92	61	3.8	61	12	<1	<1	12
	T2	79	64	3.8	68	14	<1	<1	14
	SED	30.3	2.3	0.03	2.3	0.8	-	-	0.6

Table 14.9 Effect of an inoculant/enzyme additive on the composition of ensiled forage maize

Experiment	Treatment	ODM (g/kg)	Composition (g/kg DM)				
			CP	WSC	Starch	NDF	ME (MJ/kg DM)
1	T1	259	114	10	210	476	10.5
	T2	257	120	9	214	454	10.7
	SED	4.7	5.8	0.7	10.2	8.4	0.09
2	T1	349	101	7	267	442	10.5
	T2	350	104	6	278	424	10.8
	SED	7.6	3.2	0.4	11.4	11.2	0.10

Conclusions

Treatment with the combined inoculant enzyme/additive reduced the DM loss during ensiling, and improved fermentation characteristics, nutritive value and aerobic stability. The increase in lactic acid in the treated silages can be attributed to the presence of lactic acid producing bacteria in the additive and the reduced NDF values, which are reflected in improved predicted ME values, can be attributed to the presence of cell wall degrading enzymes. An improvement in aerobic stability was evident in both experiments.

Acknowledgement

The authors would like to acknowledge financial support from Agricultural Central Trading.

Comparison of Laboratory Methods for Estimating Dry Matter Digestibility of Immature Forage Maize

P. O'Kiely, A.P. Moloney[1], J.F. O'Grady[2] and T. Keating[1]

[1]Teagasc, Grange Research Centre, Co Meath, Ireland
[2]IAWS Group Ltd., 151 Thomas St., Dublin 8, Ireland

Summary

During the ensilage of physiologically immature maize a much larger depression in dry matter digestibility in vitro (DMD) was recorded than would be predicted from the measured conservation losses or from comparisons with ensiled grass. The present experiment compared three methods for estimating the change in DMD during ensilage. The DMD of immature forage maize (<50 g/kg of crop DM present in cob) from laboratory (Experiment 1) and farm (Experiment 2) scale experiments, was estimated pre- and post-ensiling (a) by *incubation in rumen fluid (48 h) followed by acid pepsin, (b) by neutral cellulase gammanase digestion and (c) by pepsin cellulase digestion. Method (c) gave the lowest values and method (a) tended to give the highest. All methods estimated larger decreases in digestibility during the ensilage of immature forage maize than would be expected with grass.*

Introduction

Under suitable conditions forage maize can provide high yields of nutritious, readily ensilable feedstuff and is an attractive alternative to grass as a silage crop. The change in digestibility of grass or physiologically mature maize during ensilage can be negligible where good silage-making practices prevail (Dulphy and Demarquilly, 1991), whereas bad ensilage techniques can result in a considerable decrease in digestibility (Flynn, 1981). When grown under sub-optimal conditions, maize may be physiologically immature at harvesting, resulting in a forage of low starch content. The yield, nutritive value and economic value of such crops tend to be disappointing. Previous results indicated that whereas physiologically immature maize readily underwent a lactic acid dominant fermentation and had a conservation efficiency comparable to good grass silage, the change in dry matter digestibility during ensilage, as estimated *in vitro* by the technique of Tilley and Terry (1963), was greater than anticipated. The present experiments sought to test if the change was an artefact of the assay, and compared the changes as measured using this assay with two other methods.

Materials and methods

Immature forage maize (< 50 g/kg crop dry matter (DM) present in cob) was ensiled in laboratory (Experiment 1) and farm (Experiment 2) scale silos. Samples were taken at ensiling and silo opening (over 100 days ensilage), dried at 40°C for 48h, ground through a 1 mm screen, and assessed for DM digestibility by the following methods:

(a) Incubation in rumen fluid (48 h) followed by acid pepsin (48 h) (Tilley and Terry, 1963 with the modification that the final residue was separated by filtration rather than centrifugation).

(b) Neutral cellulase gammanase digestion (MAFF, 1992).

(c) Pepsin cellulase digestion (De Boever *et al.*, 1986).

Table 14.10   Comparison of laboratory methods for estimating digestibility of immature forage maize - mean (s.d.)

Stage of ensiling	Laboratory silos (Experiment 1)			Farm silos (Experiment 2)		
	Pre (n=3)	Post (n=3)	Change	Pre (n=3)	Post (n=6)	Change
Assay						
(a) DMD[1] (g/kg)	697 (5.5)	636 (11.1)	-61	762 (6.7)	693 (10.6)	-69
(b) NCGD[2] (g/kg)	643 (12.5)	571 (14.4)	-72	759 (2.9)	714 (8.3)	-45
(c) PCD[3] (g/kg)	616 (18.6)	569 (13.9)	-47	730 (8.7)	677 (18.4)	-53
SEM	7.7	14.1		3.8	5.4	
Significance	***	*		**	***	

[1] Dry matter digestibility
[2] Neutral cellulase gammanase digestibility
[3] Pepsin cellulase digestibility

Results

The mean composition of the maize at ensiling in Experiment 1 was 216 g DM/kg, 100 g crude protein/kg DM, 285 g acid detergent fibre/kg DM, 60 g ash/kg DM, 171 g WSC/kg DM, a buffering capacity of 283 mEq/kg DM and no starch, while the corresponding values in Experiment 2 were 195 g DM/kg, 134 g/kg DM, 225 g/kg DM, 61 g/kg DM, 202 g/kg DM, 333 mEq/kg DM and no starch. Silages in both experiments were well preserved with no evidence of aerobic deterioration problems. Silage fermentation characteristics in Experiment 1 were pH

3.9; 64 g lactic acid/kg DM; 32 g acetic acid/kg DM; 91 g ethanol/kg DM and 51 g NH_3-N/kg N. The corresponding values in Experiment 2 were 3.92, 88 g/kg DM; 25 g/kg DM; 22 g/kg DM and 60 g/kg N. The comparison of laboratory methods for estimating digestibility is summarised in Table 14.10. The results indicate that the Tilley and Terry technique tended to give the highest values and the pepsin cellulase technique the lowest. All three techniques estimated considerably larger decreases in digestibility during the ensilage of immature forage maize than anticipated, based on prior experience with grass.

Conclusion

The large depression recorded in digestibility during ensilage was not an artefact of the Tilly and Terry (1963) assay.

References

DE BOEVER J.L., COTTYN B.G., BUYSSE F.X., WAINMAN F.W. and VANACKER J.M. (1986) The use of an enzymatic technique, to predict digestibility, metabolisable and net energy of compound feedstuffs for ruminants. *Animal Feed Science and Technology,* **14**:203-214.

DULPHY J.P. and DEMARQUILLY C. (1991) Digestibility and voluntary intake of conserved forage. In: Pahlow G. and Honig H. (eds.) *Forage Conservation Towards 2000.* Landbauforschung Volkenrode, Sonderheft, **123**: 140-160.

FLYNN A.V. (1981) Factors affecting the feeding value of silage. In: Haresign, W. (ed.) *Recent Advances in Animal Nutrition,* 81-89, Butterworths.

MINISTRY OF AGRICULTURE, FISHERIES and FOOD (1992) Determination of neutral cellulase plus gammanase digestibility (NCGD) of feedstuffs. In: *Prediction of Energy Value of Compound Feedstuffs for Farm Animals,* Appendix II, MAFF, London.

TILLEY J.M.A. and TERRY R.A. (1963) A two-stage technique for the *in vitro* digestion of forage crops. *Journal of the British Grassland Society,* **18**: 104-111.

Effect of Freezing or Enzyme Treatment before Ensiling on the Nutritive Value of Maize Silage

U. R. Altaf, E. Owen and R.H. Phipps

*Department of Agriculture, The University of Reading,
Earley Gate, P O Box 236, Reading RG6 6AT, UK*

Summary

The changes in composition were studied in whole-crop maize ensiled in 2.5 kg laboratory silos either immediately after harvest or ensiled after freezing and thawing. The latter procedure is often used in research when large numbers of silages have to be prepared. The fresh and frozen forages were either ensiled with or without the addition of a cell-wall degrading enzyme. Freezing did not affect (P<0.05) silage pH or contents of lactic acid, neutral detergent fibre (NDF) or acid detergent fibre (ADF), but reduced (P<0.01) organic matter digestibility in vitro (OMD). Enzyme treatment decreased (P<0.01) silage pH, increased (P<0.05) lactic acid, decreased (P<0.05) NDF and decreased (P<0.05) ADF, but surprisingly, did not improve OMD. The results suggest that freezing whole crop maize before ensiling is likely to have only minor effects on pH, lactic acid, NDF and ADF, but will reduce OMD by about 40 g/kg. The enzyme used clearly increased lactic acid, reduced pH and reduced NDF and ADF, but did not improve OMD. The latter result is surprising and merits further research.

Introduction

A crop for silage should be ensiled immediately after harvesting. However, this is not always possible in research situations when a large number of laboratory-scale silos have to be prepared. Thus, in many cases, the chopped material is frozen and ensiled at a later date after defrosting. The current study was conducted to determine changes in the composition of fresh and frozen whole-crop maize, ensiled with and without a cell-wall degrading enzyme solution. It was hypothesised that freezing would not affect composition, but that treatment with enzyme would decrease cell-wall content, decrease pH and increase digestibility *in vitro*.

Materials and methods

Forage-harvested maize was divided into two portions. One 50 kg portion was placed in a deep freeze and the other split into two 25 kg lots. One lot was treated with a cell-wall degrading enzyme solution supplied by Finnfeeds International Ltd. The enzyme added, at 0.6 ml (plus 4.4 ml water)/kg forage, was applied with a hand-operated sprayer and the forage thoroughly hand-mixed. The remainder was treated with an amount of water equal to that used to dilute the enzyme solution for even distribution. The enzyme-treated and untreated forages were then ensiled in 2.5 kg capacity laboratory silos (5 silos/treatment). After 30 days, the frozen forage was defrosted at room temperature, split into two 25 kg lots and ensiled with or without enzyme treatment, using 5 silos/treatment, as before. The trial design was a randomised complete block with a 2 x 2 factorial arrangement of treatments and 5 replicates. After 300 days the silos were opened and silages assessed for pH, dry matter (DM), NDF, ADF, lactic acid and OMD *in vitro* (Tilley and Terry, 1963).

Results

The results are summarised in Tables 14.11 and 14.12. Freezing did not affect ($P<0.05$) silage pH or contents of lactic acid, NDF or ADF, but reduced ($P<0.01$) OMD (g/kg; fresh, 720; frozen 684) and there was a freezing x enzyme interaction ($P<0.01$) for DM content. Enzyme treatment decreased ($P<0.01$) NDF content and decreased ($P<0.05$) ADF content. However, surprisingly, enzyme treatment did not improve OMD.

Conclusions

Freezing whole crop maize before ensiling resulted in only minor effects on pH, lactic acid, NDF and ADF, but reduced OMD *in vitro* by about 40 g/kg. The cell-wall degrading enzyme used clearly increased lactic acid content, reduced pH and reduced NFD and ADF, but was without effect on OMD *in vitro*. The latter result is surprising and merits further research.

Table 14.11   **Effect of freezing and enzyme additive on the fermentation characteristics of ensiled forage maize**

Enzyme	Freezing	DM (g/kg)	pH	Lactic	Acetic	Propionic	Total
No	No	291	3.45	50	19	0.3	69.3
No	Yes	249	3.87	55	28	1.7	84.7
Yes	No	277	3.20	58	20	0.3	78.3
Yes	Yes	272	3.17	80	20	1.0	101.0
s.e.d		8.1	0.069	5.6	1.74	0.27	6.91

The "Lactic Acetic Propionic Total" columns are under the heading **Fermentation acids (g/kg DM)**.

Table 14.12.   **Effect of freezing and enzyme additive on the composition and nutritive value of ensiled forage maize**

Enzyme	Freezing	NDF	ADF	Lignin	Cellulose	Hemicellulose	OMD (g/kg)
No	No	433	235	30	202	198	730
No	Yes	458	279	32	211	179	695
Yes	No	383	203	29	165	179	711
Yes	Yes	405	214	34	174	192	673
s.e.d		13.1	14.6	1.5	4.3	17.1	11.9

The "NDF ADF Lignin Cellulose Hemicellulose" columns are expressed in (g/kg DM).

Acknowledgements

U.R. Altaf acknowledges a postgraduate scholarship from the Government of Pakistan. The authors are grateful to Finnfeeds International Ltd. for supporting the study.

Reference

TILLEY J.M.A. and TERRY R.A. (1963) A two-stage technique for the *in vitro* digestion of forage crops. *Journal of the British Grassland Society*, **18**: 104-111.

Genetic Variation and Effectiveness of Nitrogen Fixation of *Rhizobium meliloti* Strains Forming Nodules on Lucerne

C.M. Gandee and S.P. Harrison

The Royal Agricultural College, Cirencester, Gloucestershire, GL7 6JS

Summary

This study employed a method of genetic characterisation known as RAPD fingerprinting to address a number of questions about the status of Rhizobium meliloti *populations inhabiting the nodules of commercially grown lucerne or test soils in which lucerne might be grown.* Rhizobium *strains were isolated from nodules harvested from lucerne plants, grown in adjacent experimental plots, from either inoculated or uninoculated seed. The dry matter production of representative plants from both of these treatments were assessed. All rhizobia were characterised genetically and there was a rich diversity of* R. meliloti *in the soils tested. Inoculated plots and uninoculated plots did not differ in terms of dry matter production. It would appear that lucerne can be grown and adequately nodulated in soils with no history of cultivation and can be nodulated by indigenous rhizobia to provide a thriving commercial crop.*

Introduction

Lucerne is a perennial legume which, under low nitrogen conditions, has a necessity to form a symbiotic relationship with bacteria of the species *Rhizobium meliloti.*

Seed of legumes sown in nitrogen-deficient soils are often inoculated with rhizobia with the aim of maximising crop yields. The importance of the use of inocula for lucerne production has long been recognised (Coburn, 1906) but the dynamics of the interaction with the host plant and the indigenous rhizobial population has not been well understood.

To provide information about the relative nodulation nitrogen fixation of inoculant and indigenous rhizobia it is fundamental to be able to analyse the genetic constitution of the rhizobial populations in question. Harrison *et al.* (1992), Dooley *et al.* (1993) and Dye *et al.* (1995) used Randomly Amplified Polymorphic DNA (RAPD) fingerprints for rhizobial identification. The present study also employed this method to address questions about the status of *R. meliloti* populations inhabiting the nodules of lucerne grown in test plots.

Methods

Rhizobium strains were isolated from nodules harvested from lucerne plants growing in adjacent experimental plots which were either inoculated or uninoculated and from two commercial fields both containing soils of Cotswold Brash. The dry matter production of representative plants from both of these treatments were assessed and all rhizobia were assessed for relative genetic diversity between treatments.

Results

The use of RAPD profiling was effective in screening rhizobial population from varied sources. Amplified products within each profile varied between strains of rhizobia. From this variation in number and size of bands it was possible to identify individual strains from what could be called a "DNA fingerprint". Although strains for the most part gave rise to unique identifiable profiles, the patterns produced by several strains were very similar.

Dry weights of plants grown in inoculated and uninoculated plots did not differ (Table 14.13), suggesting that lucerne can be grown and adequately nodulated in soils with no history of lucerne cultivation. Lucerne can be nodulated by indigenous rhizobia and provide a thriving commercial crop. There would appear to be a rich diversity of *R. meliloti* in soils even where lucerne has not been grown (Table 14.14). It might, therefore, be suggested that it is not necessary to apply a commercial inoculant to lucerne seed. When one considers that many inoculants are from diverse origins and may not compete with the indigenous populations for nodulation or might not be adapted to local conditions, the use of such inocula appears less viable. It might, however, be suggested that if an inoculum strain is to be applied then it should be derived from the local population and reapplied to the field in larger numbers. If present in larger numbers an effective nitrogen fixing strain may be in a position to occupy a greater percentage of nodules than an unadapted strain from a distant origin.

Table 14.13   **Effect of inoculation of lucerne seed on seedling dry weights and on nodule scores**

	Seed treatment		
	Inoculated	Uninoculated	Significance
Mean plant dry weight (mg)	17.07	17.63	NS
Mean nodule score	1.84	2.44	p<0.01

Table 14.14   **Isolates of *R. meliloti* extracted from nodules of lucerne grown in inoculated and uninoculated plots**

Source of isolates	Number of isolates	Strains (frequency)	Observations
Inoculated plot	40	Inoculant strain (11), Ia (3), Ib (2), Ic (2), Others (22), Total (26)	Inoculant strain was present as 28% of isolates.
Uninoculated plot	38	Ua (7), Ub (3), Uc (2), Ud (2), Uk (3), Others (21), Total (26)	Ua was the same as Ib in inoculated plot.

Strain types were labelled according to their plot of origin, i.e. inoculated-I and uninoculated-U, and then given letters non-preferentially.

Conclusion

There appears to be a wide array of strains of *R. meliloti* within the soils examined. Many of these strains have undoubted potential as future inoculants both in terms of their nitrogen fixation capacity and their adaptation to UK soils. They therefore represent a valuable asset to low input agricultural systems if managed correctly. However, it might also be suggested that in many agricultural situations the use of current commercial inoculants may not result in enhanced crop growth or dry matter production.

References

COBURN, F.D. (1906) *The Book of Alfalfa*. Orange Judd Company. New York.

DOOLEY, J.J., HARRISON, S.P., MYTTON, L.R., DYE, M., CRESSWELL, A. SKOT, L. and BEECHING, J.R. (1993) Phylogenetic grouping and identification of Rhizobium species based on Randomly Amplified Polymorphic DNAs (RAPDs) profiles. *The Canadian Journal of Microbiology*. **39**, 725-730.

DYE, M., SKOT, L., MYTTON, L.R., HARRISON, S.P., DOOLEY, J.J. & CRESSWELL, A. (1995) A study of *Rhizobium leguminosarum* biovar *trifolii* populations from soil extracts using randomly amplified polymorphic DNA profiles. *The Canadian Journal of Microbiology*. **41**, 336-344.

HARRISON S.P., MYTTON L.R., SKOT L., DYE M. & CRESSWELL A. (1992) Characterisation of *Rhizobium* isolates by amplification of DNA polymorphisms using random primers. *Canadian Journal of Microbiology*. **34**, 3423-30.

The Effect of Establishment Method and Spring Plant Population on the Dry Matter Yield of First Season Stands of Lucerne (*Medicago sativa*)

G.P.F. Lane and A. Moore

The Royal Agricultural College, Cirencester, Glos GL7 6JS UK

Summary

The conclusion of a field trial commenced in 1995 is described. The objective was to test various methods of establishing lucerne under specific conditions. Plant numbers per square metre and dry matter yields from three cuts are reported. Yields were closely correlated with *spring plant numbers (P<0.01). Dry matter yields of lucerne undersown in forage maize were only just significantly lower (P<0.05) than the direct sown plots and it was concluded that in view of the extra dry matter yield obtained during the establishment year that undersowing maize with lucerne could be a viable method for establishment on a field scale.*

Introduction

The influence of establishment method on lucerne (cv. Vela) plant numbers established in the spring has been reported previously (Lane and Moore, 1996). The purpose of this short paper is to complete the picture and to give an account of the first season dry matter yields from the successfully established treatments as far as they are available.

Methods

Fresh weight yield estimates were made on three occasions (7 June, 26 July and 6 September) during 1996. The plots measured 10m x 4m and two separate square metre areas were sampled at random from each plot and weighed. Subsamples were taken for dry matter determination and dried for at least 24 hours at 102°C. After the yield estimates were taken the rest of the plots were mown on each occasion with a "Hayter" rotary mower and the residue discarded. Since some of the lucerne establishments had not been successful (undersown in spring barley on 1 June and direct sown on 30 August) not all of the treatments previously mentioned could be harvested. Those treatments that were are listed below:

1. Lucerne sown direct in late April 1995 with inoculum.
2. Lucerne sown direct in late April 1995 with no inoculum.
3. Lucerne undersown in spring barley in late April 1995.
5. Lucerne sown direct in early June 1995.
7. Lucerne undersown into established forage maize in early June 1995.

Results

The yields of dry matter are shown in Table 14.15. A regression analysis was carried out to test the correlation between the total dry matter yield from the three cuts and the spring plant population. The results are shown in Figure 14.2.

Table 14.15   Dry matter yields (t DM/ha)

Treatment	Plants/m^2	Ist cut	2nd cut	3rd cut	Total yield
1	137	7.8	2.7	1.7	12.2
2	137	8.0	2.6	1.5	12.1
3	100	5.0	1.9	1.3	8.2
5	122	7.2	2.3	1.7	11.3
7	120	7.1	2.1	1.4	10.6
LSD (P<0.05)	16	1.9	0.6	0.3	1.6

Figure 14.2   Regression of dry matter yield against spring plant population

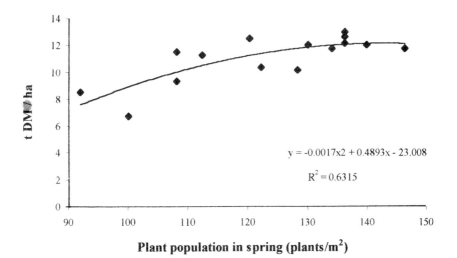

$$y = -0.0017x2 + 0.4893x - 23.008$$

$$R^2 = 0.6315$$

Plant population in spring (plants/m^2)

Discussion

After excellent first cut yields, the yields of the two subsequent cuts were disappointing. This was probably due to the exceptionally dry conditions obtaining in 1996. The soil moisture deficit calculated under grass from MORECS data for the period from late June until late September was around 120 mm. The yields obtained from Treatment 3 (lucerne undersown in spring barley) were significantly less than the other four treatments ($P<0.001$). The most probable reason for this was the reduced number of plants per square metre. Although the lucerne stand established under forage maize (Treatment 7) was thinner and yielded less than the direct sown plots, the difference was only just statistically significant ($P<0.05$). In view of the extra dry matter yield which had been obtained from the forage maize crop in the establishment year it was thought that undersowing in maize would be a viable technique for establishing lucerne.

There was a strong correlation ($P<0.01$) between spring plant number and total dry matter yield (Figure 14.2). Around 130 to 140 plants/ square metre appeared to be optimum but reasonable yields were still obtained with plant populations of 120 to 130/square metre. Significant yield losses occurred however when lucerne plant populations dropped to 100/square metre. There was no significant difference between Treatments 1 and 2, indicating that there were sufficient indigenous *Rhizobium* spp. for successful nodulation to occur.

Conclusion

Direct sowing was the best method for establishing lucerne in these conditions. Undersowing in spring barley gave poor results in dry conditions but undersowing in forage maize was shown to be a viable method for establishing lucerne in 1995. A field scale investigation was set up in 1996 to verify this claim (Lane, 1998).

References

LANE G.P.F. (1998) A novel technique for establishing lucerne (*Medicago sativa*) by undersowing in forage maize. In: Lane G.P.F. and Wilkinson J.M. (eds.) *Alternative Forages for Ruminants*. Chalcombe Publications.

LANE G.P.F. and MOORE A. (1996) Establishment strategies for lucerne. In Younie, D (ed.) *Legumes and Sustainable Farming Systems. Occasional Symposium of the British Grassland Society, no 30*, pp 322-323.

Effects of Swath Tedding During Field-Wilting of Lucerne on Dry Matter Content Variability in Wrapped Big Bale Silages

G. Borreani and E. Tabacco

Dipartimento Agroselviter, Università di Torino,
Via Leonardo da Vinci 44, 10095 Grugliasco (TO), Italy

Summary

The effects of tedding during wilting of lucerne for ensiling on dry matter (DM) content heterogeneity in swaths and in big bales silage were evaluated in 3 trials performed under highly favourable drying conditions. Variability in herbage DM content was lower for tedded than for untedded swaths before harvesting. However, 5 days after ensiling the differences were not significant and there was no effect of the variation in DM content on the fermentation quality of the silage.

Introduction

Farm-scale silage is a heterogeneous product, a habitat full of niches that differ in their chemical and microbial compositions over short distances in the silo. A large part of this heterogeneity is the effect of variation in composition of the fresh crop as well as in the mechanical treatment and in the different conditions of ensiling (Spoelstra, 1982). Tedding improves the drying rate and reduces the differences in DM content from the top to the bottom of the swath (Dernedde, 1979), but it can cause leaf loss and a reduction of nutrient concentration especially in legumes (Garthe *et al.*, 1988). The aim of this work was to evaluate the DM content variability in tedded and untedded swaths and its effect on fermentation of lucerne summer cuts ensiled as wrapped big bales.

Materials and methods

Three field experiments were carried out in the Western Po Valley in 1994 on second and third cuts of lucerne. All the forage, mowed in the morning with a 1.8 m wide roll conditioner, was left in swaths (about 20 cm high), half untedded and half tedded after about 3 hours of wilting. The forage was ensiled that same afternoon as wrapped big bales (density 150 kg DM/m^3), one for each treatment. Immediately before harvesting, the DM content of the upper and lower layers of the swaths was measured within three replications along a 40 cm length of each swath. After ensiling, the bale DM heterogeneity was evaluated by coring 50 cm deep into two replications at 0, 5 and 15 days after ensiling. Each core was split into portions of 2 to 3 cm and the DM content of each was evaluated in an oven by drying at 80°C. Fermentation analysis was done by HPLC on samples taken after 200 days of ensiling. The variability in the DM content between treatments was evaluated by testing the homogeneity of the variances using the F-test.

Results and discussion

Some crop characteristics and the hours of field drying of the tedded and untedded swaths are reported in Table 14.16. Without tedding the DM content of the lower layers was 52, 75 and 72% of the upper layers, respectively for the three experiments, while with tedding the differences were considerably reduced (Table 14.17). Immediately before harvest the homogeneity of variance of the DM content between untedded and tedded swaths was significantly different, with variance of untedded swaths about 10 times higher than tedded. One hour after ensiling, differences in DM content were significant only for the second and the third experiments, while these differences disappeared in the following 5 days of conservation. Data for chemical composition (Table 14.18) showed that all silages were well preserved with good fermentation quality, with no differences between treatments, except for higher ammonia-N content in untedded than in tedded. No butyric acid was found in any bale. This indicates no relevant clostridia development, even though the presence of niches with DM content lower than 300 g/kg (*cf.* Table 14.17) could be favourable to their growth.

Table 14.16   Some crop and drying characteristics

Experiment	1 (7 July)		2 (12 July)		3 (8 August)	
	untedded	tedded	untedded	tedded	untedded	tedded
Yield (t DM/ha)	4.2		3.3		2.5	
DM at mowing (g/kg)	155		187		171	
Crude protein (g/kg DM)	235		218		213	
Field drying period (h)	8.3	7.5	5.5	5.0	5.9	5.1

Conclusions

The high differences in DM content heterogeneity observed between tedded and untedded swaths of lucerne, almost disappeared after 5 days of conservation, owing to the improved uniformity of the untedded forage. No relevant repercussion of the different field treatments was observed on the fermentation quality of big bale silages. Although tedding is generally known to improve drying rates, under highly favourable drying conditions, lucerne could be wilted without swath tedding to reduce leaf losses, costs and damage to the crop due to the mechanical treatments.

Table 14.17 DM content (g/kg) of crop in swath (relative to upper layer in brackets) and in silage 1 hour and 5 days after ensiling. Probability of F is for testing homogeneity of variances

		Experiment 1		Experiment 2		Experiment 3	
		untedded	**tedded**	**untedded**	**tedded**	**untedded**	**tedded**
Swath at harvest	Upper layer	436 (100)	352 (100)	492 (100)	487 (100)	383 (100)	394 (100)
	Lower layer	226 (52)	274 (78)	370 (75)	450 (92)	276 (72)	355 (90)
	Variance	*13254*	*832*	*7286*	*613*	*6997*	*627*
	p (F)	*0.00*		*0.01*		*0.01*	
Silage 1 hour after wrapping	Max. value	406	409	570	530	411	417
	Min. value	261	261	396	432	270	337
	Variance	*923*	*1421*	*1152*	*491*	*1263*	*494*
	p (F)	*0.14*		*0.04*		*0.02*	
Silage after 5 days	*Variance*	*920*	*1111*	*844*	*662*	*916*	*559*
	p (F)	*0.33*		*0.16*		*0.08*	

Table 14.18   Composition of silages 200 days after ensiling

Experiment	1 untedded	tedded	2 untedded	tedded	3 untedded	tedded
DM content (g/kg)	327	331	441	481	326	364
pH	4.6	4.6	5.2	5.3	4.9	4.9
NH_3-N (g/kg TN)	100	91	80	62	105	86
Lactic acid (g/kg DM)	32	30	18	15	35	26
Acetic acid (g/kg DM)	29	25	4	8	29	21
Butyric acid (g/kg DM)	0	0	0	0	0	0
Propionic acid (g/kg DM)	0.6	0.5	0.3	0.9	1.1	0.9

References

DERNEDDE W. (1979) Treatments to increase the drying rate of cut forage. In Thomas C. (ed.) *Forage Conservation in the '80s.* Occasional Symposium No. 11, British Grassland Society, pp. 61-66.

GARTHE J.N., ANDERSON P.M., HOOVER R.J. and FALES S.L. (1988) Field test of a swath/windrow inverter. *ASAE paper No. 88*, 1549. St Joseph, Michigan.

SPOELSTRA S.F. (1982) Gasvormende clostridia in grassilage. *Bedrijfsontwikkeling jaargang*, **13**, 137-140.

Recent and On-Going Research with *Lotus* (Birdsfoot Trefoil) at IGER

A. Hopkins, D. A. Davies*, R.H. Johnson and R.D. Sheldrick

*IGER, North Wyke, Okehampton, Devon EX20 2SB; and
IGER, Bronydd Mawr, Trecastle, Brecon, Powys LD3 8RD

Summary

The advantages of **Lotus** *species as legumes for low-input situations are described.* *Trials at IGER North Wyke have shown significant variation in productivity between* **Lotus** *varieties. Yields of 7 to 10 DM t/ha were obtained from grass/Lotus swards with* **Lotus pedunculatus** *cv.* **Maku** *and with some varieties of* **L. corniculatus.** *Grass/Lotus swards sown with meadow fescue and timothy were higher yielding than those with browntop or smooth meadow grass.* **Lotus** *persistence was poor after the second harvest year. Evaluations of grass/Lotus swards under grazing are in progress.*

Introduction

Lotus is an important forage legume for extensive pastoral agriculture in many temperate regions of the world. In the UK both *Lotus corniculatus* and *Lotus pedunculatus* (syn. *L. uliginosus*) occur in semi-natural pastures, but their potential role as sown legumes for grassland remains unexploited and the species are relatively unknown to most farmers. The legumes have the potential to contribute to livestock production, particularly in marginal areas due to the following useful attributes: (1) they are nitrogen fixing legumes suitable for hay, silage or grazing; (2) they are generally more tolerant than white clover to soils that are poorly drained, droughty or of low fertility (e.g. low P and K, or extremes of pH); (3) research overseas has shown that introduction of *Lotus* into unimproved pasture can increase animal output; (4) *Lotus* herbage is non-bloating and palatable to livestock in all seasons up to flowering; (5) the *Lotus* genus includes attractive native species, important for wildlife and appropriate where biodiversity is encouraged; and (6) *Lotus* may be suited to other special situations, e.g. in agro-forestry understories.

However, *Lotus* suffers from a number of disadvantages: not least there is lack of knowledge on its potential, its management and agronomy under UK conditions, and it has been neglected by plant breeders and most other grassland researchers in the UK. These factors are reflected in its lack of use by UK farmers. There is also evidence from research overseas which shows susceptibility to some pests and diseases. Research at IGER to evaluate the agronomic potential of *Lotus* began in 1990 and has recently been extended on to other low input sites. Experimentation includes (1) a screening trial of *Lotus* cultivars, (2) a companion-grass trial, and (3) evaluations in grazed plots at contrasting sites.

Methods

(1) A trial of ten *Lotus* varieties sown with timothy grass was established in a poorly-drained silty clay loam, with low pH and low soil P, at IGER North Wyke in 1990. Harvest assessments were made under cutting with two harvests/year in 1991 and 1992.

(2) A trial of *Lotus* with four companion grass species was sown in 1991 on a moderately fertile site, and between 1992 and 1995 the effect of grass species (timothy, smooth meadow grass, browntop and meadow fescue) on two *Lotus* species (*L. corniculatus* cv. Leo and *L. pedunculatus* cv. Maku) was investigated. Plots were mown three times/year and received no fertilisers.

(3) In 1996 studies with *Lotus* were extended to (i) an upland site (IGER Bronydd Mawr) to include assessments under sheep grazing on plots in which *Lotus* plants were introduced into swards of different background fertility, and (ii) a Cotswold site under organic management, where plots of a botanically-diverse sward containing *Lotus* were sown for comparison with perennial ryegrass/white clover under mixed cutting and grazing.

Results

(1) In the variety evaluation the highest yielding variety was *L. pedunculatus* cv. Maku (7.7 t DM/ha with 44% *Lotus* in the DM), (Table 14.19), though some *L. corniculatus* varieties (e.g. Norcen and Cascade) also performed well (Sheldrick and Martyn, 1992).

(2) In the companion grass trial, highest mean yields were with meadow fescue (Table 14.20). In the second harvest year DM yields from grass/*Lotus* swards were 9.9 t/ha from meadow fescue, 9.1 t/ha from Timothy, 8.7 t/ha from browntop, and 8.0 t/ha from smooth meadow grass swards. Swards with cv. Leo were higher-yielding and had higher digestibility than with cv. Maku. DM yield and *Lotus* content declined after year 2 (Hopkins *et al.*, 1996). Satisfactory establishments were obtained on both sites of Trial (3) and assessments are in progress.

Table 14.19   Annual DM yields and quality of *Lotus* species and varieties, 1991

Species	Cultivar	*Lotus* DM (t/ha) Cut 1	Cut 2	Annual yield (t/ha) *Lotus* DM	Total DM[†]	*Lotus* quality (cut 2) DOMD	N (g/kg)
L. uliginosus	Maku	1.92	1.48	3.40	7.71	0.515	39.7
	Marshfield	0.81	1.40	2.21	5.72	0.540	36.3
L. corniculatus	Cascade	1.03	1.17	2.20	7.26	0.619	29.2
	Norcen	1.28	0.88	2.16	6.83	0.656	36.1
L. tenuis	Blenheim	0.35	1.11	1.46	6.00	0.536	33.4
L. corniculatus	Empire	0.40	0.90	1.30	5.87	-	-
L. c. ssp. arvensis	Kalo	0.44	0.86	1.30	5.90	-	-
L. corniculatus	GA-1	0.52	0.67	1.19	5.36	-	-
	AU-Dewey	0.51	0.66	1.17	6.13	-	-
	Fergus	0.33	0.79	1.12	5.52	-	-
s.e.d. (22 df)		0.349	0.322	0.597	0.758	0.0102 (8 df)	1.64 (8 df)
Level of significance		***	**	***	**	***	***

† includes grass and other plant DM

Table 14.20   Annual herbage yield (kg DM/ha) of grass/*Lotus* swards in successive years

| | Grass Species | | | | |
Lotus	*Phleum pratense*	*Agrostis capillaris*	*Festuca pratensis*	*Poa pratensis*	**Mean**
Year 1 *L. corniculatus*	8957	9489	8757	8789	8998
L. pedunculatus	6369	6924	7147	5837	6569
Mean	7663	8206	7952	7313	7784

s.e.d. & sig. *Lotus* 223.1 *** Grass species 315.5 * *Lotus* X Grass 446.2 NS

Year 2 *L. corniculatus*	8857	8679	10423	7730	8922
L. pedunculatus	9273	8769	9463	8210	8929
Mean	9065	8724	9943	7970	8925

s.e.d. & sig. *Lotus* 212.2 NS Grass species 300.1 *** *Lotus* X Grass 424.4 NS

Conclusions

Research so far has shown that sown grass/*Lotus* swards can be reasonably productive under low-input conditions in Britain, and our herbage production results compare favourably with results from grass/white clover trials under similar conditions. Opportunities to exploit low-input legume-based swards could become increasingly relevant in the future, and *Lotus* may have a role on marginal grasslands where economic returns may not justify inputs needed to maintain white clover. Further evaluations under grazing and problems of poor persistence of *Lotus* need to be addressed.

References

HOPKINS A. MARTYN T.M. JOHNSON R.H. SHELDRICK R.D. and LAVENDER R.H. (1996) Forage production by two *Lotus* species as influenced by companion grass species. *Grass and Forage Science*, **51**.

SHELDRICK R.D. and MARTYN T.M. (1992) Further developments with *Lotus* screening in the UK. *Lotus Newsletter*, **23**, 37-40.

Environment or Management? The Contribution of Clover to Forage Production in New Zealand

R.N. Baines

Royal Agricultural College, Cirencester, Glos., GL7 6JS

Summary

Eight dairy farms were surveyed in the Waikite and Waikato regions of the North Island of New Zealand to assess the relative importance of environmental and management factors in affecting the contribution of clover to forage production. Pastures contained between 17 and 30% clover (DM basis) in mid-summer. Both environmental and management factors affected the contribution of clover to forage production and output of milk. The major pasture management factors were adequate inputs of P, K and lime to match the requirements for growth of clover, short grazing rotations, conservation of excess herbage and tactical use of fertiliser N to extend the grazing season. Dairy herd management factors included high stocking rates, limited use of purchased feeds and limited reliance on home-grown conserved forage.

Introduction

Eight dairy farms were surveyed near Rotorua, New Zealand and compared to the MAF grassland dairy unit at Ruakura in the Waikato. The farms surveyed were predominantly spring calving, factory supply units with milk production coming mainly from grazed pastures with less than 10% of production conserved. The farms achieved stocking rates between 2.0 and 3.2 cows/ha and produced between 126 and 192 kg milk fat per cow (2808 to 4176 litres of milk/cow), or 322 to 448 kg milk fat/ha (7407 to 9969 litres of milk/hectare).

Grazing efficiency ranged from 65 to 73% with 7.8 to 11.7 t DM/ha per annum utilised. These levels of utilisation were achieved off predominantly ryegrass/clover pastures receiving little or no fertiliser nitrogen. This research is revisited to evaluate the relative importance of environmental factors and management techniques on the contribution white clover makes to forage production in New Zealand.

Environmental factors

The study farms were located on the North Island between Rotorua and Taopo in the Waikite region (Farms 1 to 7) and near Hamilton in the Wakato region (Farm 8). The majority of pastures surveyed were dominated by perennial ryegrass with lesser proportions of brome grass, cocksfoot, Yorkshire fog, bents and fescues. Seasonal and annual rainfall is conducive to long periods of grass growth (Table 14.21). In addition, differences in seasonal temperature do not impose any severe limitations to pasture growth, and there are only limited periods of drought. As a result, annual DM yields of up to 16 tonnes/hectare are possible in the Waikite region. At Ruakura, in the Waikato, annual yields in excess of 20 tonnes/hectare have been recorded.

Table 14.21   Climatic characteristics of farms surveyed

	Region	
	Waikite	**Waikato**
July (winter) temperature (°C)	5 to 10	5 to 10
Winter rainfall (mm)	750 to 1000	1000+
January (summer) temperature (°C)	10 to 15	10 to 20
Summer rainfall (mm)	750 to 1000	750 to 1000

Clover also grows well under these environmental conditions, its survival is enhanced due to the relatively few days of frost each winter. The majority of pastures surveyed contained between 17% and 30% clover cover (dry matter basis) at the mid-summer sampling point (Table 14.22). Paddocks on individual farms contained similar proportions of clover cover, indicating that management as well as environmental factors influenced the composition of the swards.

Table 14.22   **Profile of farms surveyed in terms of pasture characteristics, dairy herd performance and utilised metabolizable energy (UME)**

	Farm							
	1	**2**	**3**	**4**	**5**	**6**	**7**	**8**
Area (ha)	140	102	56	77	57	78	69	60
Clover (%)	27	28	17	21	22	29	24	30
N applied (kg/ha)	0	14	25	30	0	0	20	0
Herd size	385	294	102	173	139	218	182	222
LSU/ha	3.2	2.0	2.0	2.0	2.7	2.6	3.0	3.7
Milk yield per cow	2928	3023	4176	4018	3357	3567	2808	4009
Milk yield (l/ha)	9223	5955	8310	8040	9064	9274	8508	14833
UME (GJ/ha)	129	119	86	93	111	121	119	162

Management factors

The demand placed on pasture performance is directly related to the major livestock use. These survey farms, with the exception of Farms 6 and 7, had spring calving dairy units supplying milk for factory processing. Bought energy in the form of concentrates and forage made either a minor or no contribution to total energy needs, as did home-grown conserved forage in the form of hay and silage (<10%). All the farmers surveyed used feed budgeting as a management tool to transfer feed from one period to another. The main fertiliser inputs were P and K to correct soil deficiencies and stimulate clover growth, while small amounts of N were applied on some farms in the late season (Table 14.22). Much of the pasture fertility was attributed to the value of clover-fixed nitrogen at an estimated 287 to 520 kg N/ha (based on a requirement of 30 kg N per tonne of ryegrass DM).

Environmental and management factors contributing to the survival and performance of white clover on dairy farms in the North Island of New Zealand include:

Environment

- Mean summer temperatures between 10 and 20°C
- Adequate summer rainfall and limited dry periods
- Mean winter temperatures between 5 and 10oC and few days of frost
- Adequate winter rainfall

Pasture management

- High P & K inputs and lime when required
- Short grazing rotations (17-30 days) during grass flush, extended rotations (up to 60 days) as pasture growth declines
- Rank growth mown before end of season and stock clean up mown material
- Surplus forage conserved as silage or hay or moved to later period by feed budgeting
- Overgrazing prevented by off farm or sacrifice paddocks
- Tactical use of N to extend grazing season

Dairy herd management

- Spring calving herds which exert maximum grazing pressure during the grass flush
- High stocking rates giving lower milk yields per cow but high milk yields per ha
- Limited or no use of purchased energy in the form of concentrates and forage
- Limited reliance on home-grown conserved forage

Maintaining white clover: management or environment

The variation in clover contribution to the pastures and the range in UME output at a similar low level of fertiliser-N input, within a similar climatic environment (Table 14.22), suggest that both environmental and management factors contributed to the value of clover as a forage and as a source of pasture fertility.

Prediction the Metabolisable Energy Content of Whole-Crop Wheat

A.T. Adesogan [1,3], D.I. Givens [2] and E. Owen[1]

[1]*Department of Agriculture, The University of Reading, Earley Gate, Reading, Berkshire RG6 6AT*
[2]*Feed Evaluation and Nutritional Sciences, ADAS Drayton, Stratford-upon-Avon CV37 9RQ*
[3]*Now at Welsh Institute of Rural Studies, University of Wales, Llanbadarn Campus, Aberystwyth SY23 3AL*

Summary

This study examined whether laboratory-based methods predict accurately the metabolisable energy (ME) content of whole-crop wheat (WCW). In a two-year study, 26 wheat forages (cv. Slepjner, Hussar and Cadenza) were harvested at 376, 516 and 632 g dry matter (DM)/kg in Year One (Y1), and 352, 441 and 540 g DM/kg in Year Two (Y2). Forages were conserved in 200 litre barrels with or without acid additive or urea. Chemical composition and digestibility in vitro by rumen fluid pepsin (RFP) and neutral detergent cellulase plus gammanase (NCGD) were measured and calibration equations developed after near infrared reflectance spectroscopy (NIRS) of dried forages. ME content was estimated in vivo with wether sheep. RFP and NCGD predicted ME content poorly in both years ($r^2 = 0.15$). Gross energy content predicted ME accurately in both years ($r^2 = 0.58$ and 0.88), but such predictions involve autocorrelation and error transfer. ME predictions from cell wall ($r^2=0.06$ and 0.46) and ethanol ($r^2= 0.01$ and 0.56) contents were significantly ($P<0.05$) affected by year of harvest. NIRS ($r^2 = 0.68$) was the most accurate method for predicting the ME content of WCW, but future work with larger data sets is needed to validate its potential.

Introduction

Public attitudes and expense encourage the replacement of forage evaluation *in vivo* by non-invasive, laboratory-based techniques. This study assessed the accuracy of predicting the metabolisable energy (ME) content of whole-crop wheat (WCW) by laboratory assays.

Materials and methods

In a two-year study, 26 wheat forages (cv. *Slepjner, Hussar* and *Cadenza*) were harvested at 376, 516 and 632 g dry matter (DM)/kg in Year One and 352, 441 and 540 g DM/kg in Year Two (Cuts 1, 2 and 3 respectively). Forages were conserved in 200 l barrels with or without 'Maxgrass' additive (Trouw (BP) Nutrition, UK Ltd.) (5, 4 and 3 litres/tonne fresh weight to cuts 1, 2 and 3 respectively). Urea was applied at target rates of 20 or 40 g/kg DM to Cuts 2 and 3. Composition of silages was measured and digestibility determined *in vitro* using rumen fluid/pepsin (RFP; Tilley and Terry, 1963) and neutral detergent cellulase plus gammannase digestibility (NCGD; Dowman, 1993) techniques on freeze-dried, milled (1 mm) samples. Forages were given to four wether sheep at the maintenance level of feeding for 10 days, after which diet digestibility and urine energy losses were determined over 10 days. Metabolisable energy (ME) was calculated using predicted energy losses as methane (Blaxter and Clapperton, 1965). Dried forage samples were scanned using near infrared reflectance spectroscopy (NIRS) and calibration equations for ME developed. Corrections for volatiles lost during oven-drying were made (Dulphy and Demarquilly, 1981) and values expressed on a corrected DM (CDM) basis.

Results and discussion

Neither chemical composition nor digestibility *in vitro* consistently and accurately predicted ME content. Gross energy (GE) content was consistently the best predictor (Table 14.23), but using GE in ME prediction involves autocorrelation and the possibility of transfer errors. Predicting ME from ethanol is preferable, but the prediction accuracy in Year One was low. Some multivariate equations were more accurate than the monovariate equations in Table 14.23, but none was consistently accurate across years. NIRS provided the most promising prediction of ME content though the small population size used precluded the development of validation equations.

Table 14.23   Performance of the best equations for predicting the ME content (MJ/kg DM, y variate) of 26 whole-crop wheat forages from independent variables (g/kg CDM or as stated)

Predictor (x variate)	Year One (12 forages)			Year Two (14 forages)			Effect of year of harvest[a]
	r^2	Equation	s	r^2	Equation	s	
GE (MJ/ kg CDM)	0.58	-6.09 + 0.858 x	0.49	0.88	-2.93 + 0.726 x	0.64	***
NDFA [b]	0.06	8.31 + 0.003 x	0.73	0.46	1.29 + 0.020 x	1.33	**
NCGD	0.05	8.76 + 0.0013 x	0.74	0.14	20.5 - 0.016 x	1.69	*
RFP	0.05	6.20 + 0.0056 x	0.73	0.01	14.8 - 0.006 x	1.81	**
Ethanol	0.01	9.45 + 0.004 x	0.74	0.56	10.3 + 0.028 x	1.20	**

NIRS[c] $R^2 = 0.68$ s.e. of calibration = 0.539 Important wavelengths 1516, 1756, 2332 nm

[a] * $P<0.05$ ** $P<0.01$ *** $P<0.001$
[b] Neutral detergent fibre + amylase
[c] Data from both years were collated to increase the population size and enhance development of the equation

Conclusions

Digestibility *in vitro* and chemical composition predict the ME content of WCW poorly. NIRS is a more accurate tool for predicting the ME content of WCW but future work must use larger data sets to validate the potential of NIRS.

Acknowledgements

This programme was funded within the LINK Programme 'Technologies for Sustainable Farming Systems' by Agricultural Genetics Co. Ltd, BOCM Pauls, Dalgety Agriculture, Hi Spec Engineering Ltd, ICI Nutrition, J Bibby Agriculture Ltd, Maize Growers Association, Milk Marketing Board of England & Wales, Ministry of Agriculture, Fisheries & Food, Rumenco, Trouw (BP) Nutrition UK Ltd & Zeneca Seeds UK Ltd.

References

BLAXTER K.L. and CLAPPERTON J.L. (1965) Prediction of the amount of methane produced by ruminants. *British Journal of Nutrition*, **19**, 511-521.

DOWMAN M.G. (1993) Modifications to the neutral detergent cellulase digestibility method for the prediction of the metabolisable energy of compound feedstuffs containing palm kernel meal. *Journal of the Science of Food and Agriculture*, **61**, 327-331.

DULPHY J.P. and DEMARQUILLY C. .(1981) Problèmes particuliers aux ensilages. In: Demarquilly C. (ed.) *Prevision de la Valeur Nutritive des Ruminants*. Versailles: INRA, pp. 81-104A.

TILLEY J.M.A. and TERRY R.A. (1963) A two stage technique for the *in vitro* digestion of forage crops. *Journal of the British Grassland Society*, **18**, 104-111.

Chapter 15

Do Alternative Forages have a Future?
A Concluding Discussion

D. E. Beever

Centre for Dairy Research, Department of Agriculture,
The University of Reading, Earley Gate, Reading RG6 6AT

After a most exciting, informative and varied meeting with respect to the papers which have been presented, it is quite a thankless and definitely impossible task to provide a coherent summary. Nonetheless, I do believe that today has provided us with some opportunities and it is these that I wish to focus upon as we attempt to move forwards with respect to the provision of high-quality alternative forages for ruminants.

Undoubtedly many of us in the audience are already converts to the value of legumes, but we have been saying as much for over 20 years and look where we have got to in that time. Wherever we have convictions regarding the value of legumes, the time for talking amongst ourselves is over and we must get out there and start to preach what we genuinely believe in. In this respect we could have had no better start to the day than the visions of the 'prophet', Gordon Newman, who amply showed us just how good many other countries thought legumes were, yet our annual sowings of legumes amount to only 2% of all the legume seed exported by New Zealand. Gordon also warned us of the importance of establishment, the choice of seed especially in relation to susceptibility to disease and the overall need to manage the crop, whilst taking delight in the 'anti-legume' lobby which has been successfully raged by those with other vested interests. Although it was towards the end of his talk and possibly missed by many, it is prudent to recall that Gordon did attempt to provide some outline of where future research effort was required, drawing particular attention to the need to control bloat and the importance of understanding how legumes are utilised differently from grasses, especially in relation to their degradation within the rumen. He also raised the issue of legume conservation as silage, and warned the audience that when it's good it's very good indeed, but when it's bad it's horrid, indicating that the predictability of legume silage making needs to be improved.

In a no nonsense way Frank Moffat did an excellent job in confirming by practical experience what in essence was the message from Gordon. With the amount of legume that they are growing on an annual basis, it was clear to all in the audience that legumes are working for them and they would have great hesitation in changing what is clearly a good system. Four crops per annum may not be achievable by all, but when you put conservation and possible grazing options together, it is apparent that the level of animal production that can be achieved from legumes can be quite considerable.

In addressing the important issue of establishing legumes, and in particular the potential of undersowing in crops such as maize, Gerry Lane was clearly aware of the concern expressed by many that one major problem of legumes is the poor levels of production generally experienced in the year of establishment. Undersowing of legumes in maize may not be the ideal option for all farmers, especially where the maize harvest can be delayed by unfavourable weather conditions, but Gerry was open about the possible problems of compaction, a point which had been made in the previous talk, and left us to ponder that with yields of 12 tonnes DM/ha in the first full year of production his approach may be an attractive proposition for some.

Whilst recognising where flash dried forages fitted into the farming practices adopted by Hanford plc., I remain to be convinced that we are on the edge of a resurrection of dried forages for ruminants. Artificial dehydration of forages was 'in vogue' in the 1970s, but increasing oil prices saw several crop driers leave the business. However, a significant number have remained and, with the present UK market at 100,000 tonnes per annum, continue to produce high-quality products. As to the future for such feeds, it is difficult to predict, but with removal of meat and bone meal from the market, increasing concerns over proteinaceous feeds derived from genetically modified crops (maize, soya) and some public anxiety over the continued use of fishmeal, it may be that the market for dehydrated forages will show some growth over the next decade. It is evident that there is a demand for artificial dried lucerne, as significant quantities of dried lucerne are being imported from France. Dried forages should be provided on the basis of high-quality protein, with significant levels of ruminally undegradable protein, with the additional attributes of being environmentally friendly and safe.

Developing this theme further, Richard Phipps considered the role of legumes in the diet of dairy cows, as a complement to maize and a replacement for grass silage. Richard reminded us that it was 15 years ago that MAFF said there was no future in maize and that all research on maize should be terminated. This was a poor prediction of what has happened in the intervening years, and thus there may be a parallel message here for legumes. Funding bodies are slowly coming to the idea that there are options other than grass, but whilst some research is now being funded, there is a lack of co-ordination in the programmes that are being considered. Against an estimate that 1×10^6 ha of land in the UK is suitable for growing lucerne, it is concerning that currently only 20×10^3 ha are grown. Richard's study using dried lucerne as a replacement for grass silage, in a diet based on maize silage and concentrates confirmed the intake potential of legumes and concluded that an increase of 100g/d milk protein at the expense of 90g/d milk fat was achievable. Consider the economics of this, not only in terms of the increased value of milk protein but also the quota litrage that such decisions would mean to you, and all of it can be achieved without resorting to concentrates, feed additives or the like.

The paper on white clover presented by Alan Hopkins consolidated what has been known for several years with respect to the benefits in animal performance which can be achieved by increasing the contents of white clover in ryegrass dominant leys, emphasising the important contribution from nitrogen fixation. Clover is characterised by high protein and low structural carbohydrate contents. These attributes contribute to significantly improved forage intakes, in part related to a more rapid degradation of feed in the rumen. Hopkins developed this theme further

149

and concluded with rather convincing evidence that well managed grass/white clover swards should be considered as financially viable alternatives to the continued use of high fertiliser N applications.

Oliver Dowding was invited to take a similar focus on red clover, but chose to use the opportunity to address the use of this legume within an organic farming scenario. He clearly has great passion in his beliefs, but it was disappointing that he did not present a wider view of the niches where red clover can be used to advantage.

Robin Hill probably faced the most difficult, yet potentially most rewarding task of all speakers at the Conference. To those who have experience of sainfoin, its value as a ruminant feed needs no elaboration. With high protein levels, coupled with significant amounts of tannin, it is a non-bloating legume and data from previous Hurley studies confirmed that the dietary N is used more efficiently by the animal. But extensive research data on sainfoin is not available, and the situation is no better with respect to the sainfoin varieties which are available. It is regrettable but I suspect the use of sainfoin in the UK will not increase dramatically, with its potential never being achieved.

Widening the debate to other forages, the paper of Chapple *et al.* presented by Mervyn Davies examined the role of ensiled fodder beet as an alternative to maize silage and established that satisfactory rates of animal performance can be achieved. From the data presented, it was evident that harvesting in order to minimise soil contamination remains a potential problem and this could be a major limitation to any increase in its use within the UK.

Extending the theme on alternatives, Dr Vipond considered ensiled kale in the 'Scottish system', but drew concern from the audience over the low DM content of most ensiled crops, the costs of production on a DM basis (ensiled kale is not a cheap crop) and excessive estimates of ME content, given that the ash content of ensiled kale may be in excess of 120g/kg DM. Some believe the kale revolution is about to begin, whilst others see its potential to be more limited - perhaps only time will provide the answer.

Finally in this section, Dr Jones considered the potential of mixed grass/legume:cereal mixtures for ensiling in large bales, but lack of data, and a suspected low content of legume in many of the crops examined, meant that it was difficult to draw conclusions from this study.

The final two papers provided excellent summaries of the day's proceedings with issues concerning the economics of forage production and the potential of grass being firmly established in the first paper by Derek Gardner. Grass is not cheap, especially if ensiled and more suitable, often cheaper alternatives do exist, but should only be grown where they are well suited to the environment and the farming enterprise. Whole-crop wheat was seen as a valuable 'insurance crop' but was likely to be limited by its relatively modest ME value despite good intake characteristics. However there are now so many opportunities with respect to legumes, as discussed by John Bax especially for the grazing animal but whilst many legumes are difficult to ensile, serious consideration should be given to lucerne, either clamped or as big bales.

In conclusion, a highly successful day which clearly developed the many opportunities that exist for livestock farmers who are faced with eroding financial margins (e.g. reduced milk prices), increased product specification (e.g. increased milk protein contents), reduced feed availability (e.g. protein supplements) and increased fixed costs. However the research effort is fragmented, kale silage and fodder beet being clear examples of such. We need collectively to face the market by:-

i)   Defining it;
ii) Defining the animals we will be using to meet it;
iii) Defining the feeds available (better feedstuff analyses);
iv) Increasing the use of cheaper home grown feeds.

In this respect it is regrettable that potential research funders were not present at this meeting, especially given MAFF's stated intentions in these regards.